STORIES JESUS LOVED TO TELL

Daniel D. Oravec

DEDICATION

To my parents, George and Cecelia Oravec,
Who never heard the words "unconditional love"
But embodied them...
From a grateful son

...And to my grandchildren
Who, when I started this little book, were in my thoughts:
Katy Oravec, Rachel Petrie, Carrie Oravec, Matthew Petrie
and Tim Petrie
From a grandfather who could not love them more.

TABLE OF CONTENTS

PREFACE

Joy and privilege best describe my forty-four years as a pastor. Two years after my first retirement, a bonus came my way in an opportunity to serve a small church on a part-time basis. Andrea was my only confirmation student. It was a perfect time to set aside the conventional materials used in instruction and try something new. I chose the parables of Jesus to study with Andrea. It was a good choice.

Following my second retirement, my son David, also a Lutheran pastor, asked me to teach an adult course at the church he was serving, using the parables as the theme, which I did. Later on, I taught a similar adult class at the Chautauqua Institute in New York State. By this time I was totally captive to the stories of Jesus. It seemed a shame to either box or burn all my notes. Thus the idea for this little book was born. While initially meant for a teen-ager, the content had become broader and more inclusive after teaching the adult classes.

I believe there is no better way to know the heart and mind of Jesus than to study his parables. They stand as the core and keynote of his teachings. When we read his stories with an open heart and mind, they tell us what Jesus most desired to communicate.

I call this book *Stories Jesus Loved to Tell* because I believe he truly loved to describe, through the stories, the kingdom of God and to convey God's message of unconditional love.

INTRODUCTION

If we knew nothing about Jesus except the stories he loved to tell, what would we learn about him? If we had no record of his life, no gospels, no creeds—nothing but his stories—what would we discover? The more I thought about this tunnel-vision approach to writing this book, the more intrigued I became. The parables were stories that were remembered and written; I believe they reflected the heart and mind of Jesus. His desire was to tell people about God and His kingdom and what life in the kingdom was all about.

A parable is an ancient method of teaching, a story from life with an eternal meaning. It is a story that has a single message to describe life with God. When I was a teen-ager I learned a simple definition that is hard to beat: A parable is an "earthly story with a heavenly meaning." The word "parable" literally means "to throw alongside." In this case, alongside a well-known life story is a central, abiding, and eternal truth. I use the words parable and story interchangeably throughout these pages.

Stories Jesus loved to tell: The gospels tell us that Jesus never taught without using parables to illustrate his thoughts, and that his loyal followers loved to hear them.

Although the stories seem simple enough, they are not. Jesus was suggesting a new way for people's lives. Much of what he said was different from what they had been taught. To truly understand the parables, it is necessary to be in tune with the storyteller and to catch his spirit. People of the establishment were not in tune with Jesus and, as a result, sought to discredit him. Jesus taught a way that was different from obedience and sacrifice. He talked about a father and his two sons and the unheard-of love and forgiveness that the father expressed.

The heart of the stories was the kingdom of God. Jesus never directly stated what the kingdom was. Rather, he stated what it was like. Then he would illustrate with one of his earthly stories.

Most significantly, he said the kingdom of God is within you. The kingdom is not a future state, but a present reality. It is now. We are able to identify it in our every act. In every waking moment we live it. The kingdom is not a realm of morality. It is a realm of unconditional love. You do not pay admission through good works or obeying the letter of the law. To become part of the kingdom, therefore, is not putting obedience first, but unconditional love first. Kingdom living, a term I use often in these pages, is to be in communion with the heart and mind of Jesus.

For those who believe that Jesus is the embodiment of God-come-among-us, his stories should have great power and significance. They answer the perpetual questions of humankind: "What's it all about, why am I here, how am I to live...?" Proclaimed throughout the parables is the good news that Jesus described and embodied, that of God's unconditional love. In this love we become new creatures, new persons. St. Paul says it well: "I show you a new way." It was the way of love.

When we read the first chapter of John's gospel, we are introduced to a description of this man Jesus. The gospel says: *In the beginning was the Word and the Word was with God and the word was God. In him was life and the life was the light of men and the light goes on shining and darkness has not put it out. And the word was made flesh and came to dwell among us.*

"Logos" is Greek for "word." In the original Greek it meant reason, wisdom, and, my favorite definition, "the controlling principle of the universe." Thus, if we believe in Jesus as the embodiment of God, we may also claim that his words describe the heart and essence of the universe. In him is the ultimate light. He is the bringer of salvation.

A number of years ago I was looking up the definition of the word "salvation." The definitions included deliverance; preservation; a safe return home after a trip; a guarantee of security and bodily health; and being saved from captivity, sin and trouble in general. One definition jumped off the page at me. It was that salvation means wholeness. In Jesus, the Christ, we are able to find the wholeness of our lives.

I've always had difficulty with the ransom theory of the atonement—that God demanded a ransom, his son, for the forgiveness of sin. It never made sense to me that the one we call "Love" would need or demand a ransom. The love of God never excludes, never judges. What did make sense was that Jesus saved us from being other than the creatures that God created us to be. Forgiveness and total acceptance are implied in unconditional love. God's very nature is love, and that never changes. To me, nothing is more exciting in life than this thought.

When we accept that Jesus is the logos of God, we also confess that he is the ultimate benchmark for all of life. A benchmark is used by craftsmen and engineers for measuring. It's a reference point or a standard that helps in the work being done. For us, then, Jesus is the benchmark for the living of our lives. He supersedes all else.

FOREWORD

My husband, Daniel Oravec, died in January of this year, having completed most of these chapters. The remaining few were in their second draft stage, easy to finish. He managed this by working steadily during his remaining months, until he could no longer sit at his typewriter.

As I began transcribing Daniel's typewritten chapters into a Word document, I came across a few repeated terms and phrases that puzzled me. At the time, I asked Daniel about them. What he told me was somewhat different from my initial impressions. Given the possibility that his readers might also find the terms confusing, I've taken Dan's words to me as well as definitions he offered throughout the chapters to highlight four key themes in his book.

First is God. Dan uses many different names for God: "Heavenly Father," "the Eternal," "our creator,"

"Abba," and even "Daddy." To me he simply explained that God is love. I believe he says it best in Chapter 16: "We learn to love and accept ourselves and we are then empowered to reach out and love all others. It is thus we are created in the 'image of God.'" Although he often refers to God as "he," I came to believe that Dan saw God, or love, as a force beyond our comprehension.

Second is "unconditional love." We are recipients of God's eternal love and forgiveness without condition. Again, these words from Chapter 16: "When we know ourselves to be loved and accepted, we are able to discover the God within us; we are able to give ourselves in love to all others." Further, in Chapter 11 he writes, "To love unconditionally also means unconditional acceptance and forgiveness." Dan truly felt that unconditional love is the controlling principle of the universe.

Third is "coming to oneself." Dan describes very explicitly what he means by this in his first chapter, "Struck by the Word," but the above phrase, "to discover the God within us," pretty well sums it up. Once one "comes to oneself," the journey has just begun.

Fourth is "kingdom living," also known as, simply, "the kingdom," and even "heaven." Dan stresses throughout these pages that kingdom living means living in a relationship with God, receiving unconditional love and extending that love to all others. In chapter 8 he states that "The kingdom is not some distant event that we need to prepare for but the eternal now...The kingdom of heaven is a present reality." In his introduction he notes that "In every waking moment we live it."

For Dan, *Stories Jesus Loved to Tell* was a labor of love. It was a culmination of his life-long search for meaning. Making no attempt to be scholarly or academic, he presents in these pages his own interpretation of the parables and his hope for the world.

Edwinna Bernat Oravec
October 2015

CHAPTER 1

STRUCK BY THE WORD

Over my desk hangs a plaque that has these words of St. Augustine. It reads:

> O Lord, thou didst
> Strike my heart
> With thy word
> And I loved thee.

These have always been special words for me for they remind me of one afternoon in my life.

It was a sleepy Sunday afternoon in the fall of my second year in seminary at Gettysburg. The dorm was nearly empty. I was reading St. Paul and Soren Kierkagaard for a class assignment. I don't remember anymore exactly what I was reading. I only know that suddenly I was overcome with a sense of being loved and accepted as never before.

Later I would read the words of John Wesley about an experience he described as, "My heart was strangely warmed." His words resonated with me. Only in retrospect do I claim that my heart had been struck by God's word. I only know that a powerful sense of joy and love came over me.

I was nurtured in a Christian family and never doubted that I was loved and accepted. Until that afternoon, however, being loved by God was not a powerful, conscious reality in my life. After that day I was never the same. From that moment to the present, the experience marked my entry into a loving relationship with my Maker and my Lord. The living out of my days has brought joy and sorrow, challenges and opportunities; but the experience of that Sunday afternoon has remained a sustaining reality.

Being struck by the word of God is to be touched with joy. It is to know God as the Good Shepherd, who seeks until he finds, like the father in the parable of the prodigal son. His love is unconditional. There are no tests to pass, no requirements to be met. It is only for us to accept and live that life of love. When we are touched by this love, all of life changes. It's not unlike finding the love of your life, the kindred soul you've always longed for and sought. When you find her or him, life becomes new and different. Just a few days ago I heard a young man named Kevin say, "There was life before Phoebe, but since she's come into my life, everything is different." When struck by the living word, all things become new.

As mentioned above, how this happens is different for each person. For some, it happens almost instantaneously; others may experience it imperceptibly, incrementally over a period of time. It may come by hearing or reading the good news from Jesus of God's unconditional love. It may come through another person who loves us, and in that other, we meet God. For some it comes in the wonder and awe of a newborn child or in the beauty of some great piece of music. We are touched and enter a new realm or a new paradigm.

Jesus said, "The kingdom of heaven is within you." It is for us to ponder and seek, to be open to receive and to identify the touch when it comes.

In the depths of our being we discover ourselves; it is within ourselves that we encounter the abiding presence of our Maker and Lord. It is here that we are set free to accept ourselves, dark side and all, as being loved unconditionally. It is here that we are born anew. It is here that we delight in the will and way of God for ourselves. We are saved to be ourselves as God's creatures and to grow into His image.

CHAPTER 2

JESUS HAD A FAVORITE STORY

Jesus had a favorite story and I know what it is. Well... kind of... I feel I know it because it's my favorite story, too. I feel so strongly about this parable that for anyone to miss the power and promise of it is to miss what Jesus came to share. In the story of a father and his two sons, we experience what I believe is the very heart of the gospel, God's unconditional love.

No story in my life has had a greater impact on me. It is a beautiful story that reaches into the depths of my being. It speaks so powerfully of unconditional love that it draws me into the heart of the eternal.

I believe Jesus must have told the story over and over again. It's often referred to as the "Parable of the Prodigal."

How important it is for us to remember the details of this story as it appears in the 15th chapter of Luke's gospel, verses 11-24! Read it again:

Then Jesus said: "A certain man had two sons. And the younger of them said to his father, 'Father, give me the portion of goods that falls to me.' So he divided to them his livelihood. And not many days after, the younger son gathered all together, journeyed to a far country, and there wasted his possessions with prodigal living. But when he had spent all, there arose a severe famine in that land, and he began to be in want. Then he went and joined himself to a citizen of that country, and he sent him into his fields to feed swine. And he would gladly have filled his stomach with the pods that the swine ate, and no one gave him anything.

"But when he came to himself, he said, 'How many of my father's hired servants have bread enough and to spare, and I perish with hunger! I will arise and go to my father, and will say to him, "Father, I have sinned against heaven and before you, and I am no longer worthy to be called your son. Make me like one of your hired servants."'

"And he arose and came to his father. But when he was still a great way off, his father saw him and had compassion, and ran and fell on his neck and kissed him. And the son said to him, 'Father, I have sinned against heaven and in your sight, and am no longer worthy to be called your son.'

5

"But the father said to his servants, 'Bring out the best robe and put it on him, and put a ring on his hand and sandals on his feet. And bring the fatted calf here and kill it, and let us eat and be merry; for this my son was dead and is alive again; he was lost and is found.' And they began to be merry."

I hear Jesus saying as he concluded the story to yet another gathering, "And that's the way it is in the kingdom of God." Here I write a somewhat modified version.

There was a man who had two sons and he loved them both. The elder of the two boys was by all standards a good boy. He was hard-working, obedient and had good manners. Indeed, he never gave his parents cause for concern. The younger son, on the other hand, was restless, felt abused by his brother, and had a rebellious spirit. He could hardly wait to leave home and be out on his own.

No sooner had he turned eighteen than he announced that he was leaving home. He and some of his friends were moving to the big city and taking an apartment together. His parents were disappointed but not surprised. They had been worried about him for some time.

Before leaving, the son approached his father and demanded his share of his inheritance. He said, "Father, I want my share of the property and I want it now and not when I'm too old to enjoy it. " This was an unheard of request. It was, in a way, wishing for the death of his father. To the boy's amazement, his father agreed. That very day the son went out and sold his share and filled his pockets with the cash. He was pleased with himself.

The day for his departure finally arrived. The son was beside himself with excitement. Home had been such a drag. He expected the day to be unpleasant, even ugly, but his parents were subdued. His mother helped him complete his packing and straightened his jacket. It was then he noticed that her eyes were red. Something deep within him refused to notice beyond a slight catch in his voice. It was time; his friends were on their way.

His father, his face strangely frozen, walked with him carrying two of his boxes. When they arrived at the driveway, they stood awkwardly silent. Then as the car bearing his friends appeared, the father turned to his son and said, "My son, I will always love you and this will always be your home." With that he kissed his son and walked back to the house.

As he was leaving, the younger son saw his brother out of the corner of his eye. Now his "goody two-shoes" brother wouldn't have him to make fun of and push around. He couldn't wait to get away from "Mr. Perfect." As he ran to meet his friends, he heard his brother's last words: "Good riddance to the spoiled brat." He jumped into the car with his friends and they were off.

The big city didn't disappoint him: Good friends, money to burn, all his dreams becoming reality. He was pleased that he had pulled it all off. The chicks were hot and willing, and why not? He had new wheels, great clothes, and could afford the best. What's more, he was lavish in his sharing.

Time passed. He and his buddies lived the good life. "It doesn't get any better than this" was their mantra. Home was a distant memory. When he did remember, the agenda of the day quickly crowded out thoughts of home.

The first year flew by. The second year brought some subtle changes. The group wasn't the same. Perhaps living together was a major factor. They still laughed a lot and intoned their mantra, but his friends were moving on. Some found girlfriends; some got jobs as their money was running out.

The third year saw the bottom drop out. His money was almost gone. The friends were scattered. He couldn't afford the high living any more. It seemed things couldn't get worse. The economy went flat and the job market dried up. No one seemed to care whether he was alive or dead. No one was there for him. Because he had no credit, he was soon evicted from his apartment. He wandered the streets, bitter and dejected. Finally in desperation, he took a job on a local farm feeding the pigs. At one point he was so hungry, even the pigs' slop looked good. He wondered aloud, "Was it worth it?" He considered ending it all. Anything was better than this miserable life.

As he took a rest behind the pigsty pondering all this, a startling image occurred to him: Home! He sat up, blinking his eyes in wonderment. The thought of going home had never entered his head until that moment. "Home," he whispered. "I could go home," he thought. "Maybe my father would take me on as one of the hired hands. They had a pretty good life—a place to sleep, food to eat. Maybe, just maybe..."

"I'll tell Dad how wrong I was and that I am sorry I went against him and his wishes for me, as well as against God's laws." He was moving as he thought. Even though the lack of food had taken its toll on his strength, his body had a new burst of energy. He was filled with hope for the first time.

In spite of his weakness, the journey toward home was charged with lightness. He didn't look back, but was enthralled with his vision of home. He was excited to be going home, the place just a few years ago he could not wait to leave.

The prodigal moved with a hope borne in his memory, a memory of home and his father. He saw his father in a new light as he remembered things about him that had never before registered. He had no expectation of coming back as a son, only as a hired hand. The simple thought that he would be home with his father filled him with happiness.

He was in pain but hardly noticed. He limped but never stopped. He rehearsed the words he would say to his father. Tears came when he reflected and understood for the first time the pain he had caused his father and mother.

Back home, the young man's parents had a daily ritual. It had begun shortly after he left. Together they would stand by the window that gave the best view of the road. One could see for several miles. Beyond the road was the big city, the place that held their son. They hated the place and all it stood for. They prayed, held each other and shed tears. They had aged over the years more quickly than normal. Life moved on but they were conscious of the hole in their hearts created by the absence of their younger son. Yearning and hoping, they continued their vigil. The years seemed an eternity, but they came daily, waiting and watching. They both feared the worst, that their beloved son was dead.

One afternoon the father sat alone, half asleep, keeping his vigil. As he nodded, his eyes caught a speck of movement far up the road. In an instant, a deep instinct sounded and awakened him. He bounded to his feet, knocking over his chair as his old body moved as it had not done in years. He ran down the stairs, running and shouting.

The prodigal son rounded a bend and suddenly his father's farm came into view. The place he had grown to hate was now creating such emotions that he was overwhelmed by them. He stopped to take it all in. He was about to rehearse the words he would say to his father when he was startled by a sight that baffled him. He saw a group of men running toward him. Fear gripped him as he thought that he might be punished. He was transfixed as he observed in wonder the scene before him. The wonderment turned to disbelief and dismay as he noticed that the figure leading the running men was his father. He was laughing and crying and half-way dancing, and yelling over and over, "He's alive! He's alive!"

While the son's senses were still reeling, he was being hugged and kissed. He attempted to say the rehearsed words, "Father, I'm sorry..." But his father wasn't listening. He was shouting orders: "Bring him clean clothes and new shoes for his poor feet. Prepare a feast. Call all the neighbors and invite them to a party of celebration. For this my son was dead and is alive."

The vision of God that Jesus gave his listeners in this story astonished them. It was so very different from all they had learned and experienced. Their teachers had led them to see a demanding God, a God to be feared.

For his listeners to hear Jesus tell that there was no absolute requirement to receive God's unconditional love was a revelation. Little wonder that the officials of the religious establishment were upset. All they had taught was being challenged.

Some two thousand years later, the power of the story of the man and his son remains, for me, at the center of all Jesus taught. If we could but remain faithful to this story, if we would allow it to speak to every fiber of our being and then act accordingly toward others, the world would indeed be the enchanted land, the place of love, joy, and peace.

I would like to point out a few, highlights of the story.

First, the phrase, "He came to himself." When we leave home as the prodigal did or leave God and live in the far country, we are less than whole. We are at best a divided self, seeking to fill the void that the loss of home and God creates. The prodigal hit bottom. He was alone in every way. Then, miracle of miracles, "He came to himself." He remembered home and his father and discovered a new hope. He turned away from the life he had led and started for home. We could say he had an insight about himself and his life, and he moved toward the remembered vision.

Second, Jesus represents God as Father. The word he uses is "Abba" or "Daddy," a word of intimacy, trust and care.

Third, The father's rejoicing. The father is filled with joy at the sight of his son. He throws a party to celebrate. He makes no demands of the son as a condition to his returning. The words rejoicing and celebrating are the words that describe God at the homecoming of his children and all those who are members of the kingdom.

Fourth, the elder brother's choice. As we shall see in Chapter 7, the prodigal's elder brother refused to join the celebration for his brother's return. It is possible for us to miss out on the unconditional love of the Father by refusing to "go in." There is no exclusion in God's love. Exclusion comes only when we, like the elder brother, refuse to accept the new paradigm of unconditional love and forgiveness.

There is a contemporary story of a modern-day prodigal and his return home. It involves a rebellious young man. He was angry and acted out that anger in all parts of his life. He left home seeking total independence. Things went from bad to worse and he ended up in jail.

During his jail sentence he learned to appreciate himself and his family. The time finally came for his release from prison. He had a longing to be reunited with his parents and his brothers and sisters. He had had no contact with them for years, but he decided to write a letter home.

"Dear Mom and Dad," he wrote, "I know I've made a mess of my life. I've been in jail for several years and have had a lot of time to think. I'm really sorry for the way I've been and how I treated you. I would like to come home but I wouldn't blame you if you don't want to see me. This coming Tuesday I'll be getting out and taking the train that goes by the back yard of our house. If it's okay for me to stop, put a dish towel on the clothesline. If I don't see one, I'll just stay on the train and pass by."

On Tuesday the boy was released and he boarded the train. He was apprehensive about the dish towel, and steeled himself to pass on by in its absence. As the train approached his house, he was overwhelmed to see not one towel, but dozens of towels, sheets, tablecloths and pillow cases billowing from every inch of the clothesline, saying, "Welcome home…"

—∢ ∤—

No story has had a greater impact on me than the story of the man and his two sons. It continues to reduce me to tears, an effect that has been long-standing. When I would be reading the story in worship or preaching on the subject, it was always necessary for me to prepare myself, to contain my feelings beforehand lest I break into tears.

An illustration of the powerful effect this parable had on me occurred some years ago while I was on a trip to St. Petersburg, Russia. We were touring the magnificent Hermitage Museum when the guide led us to Rembrandt's original painting of *The Prodigal.* I was not aware that the painting was in the museum and was thrilled at the sight of it. I saw the son kneeling before the father--ragged clothes, torn and tattered sandals on his feet--a broken creature. In spite of the wretched condition of the young man, the painting conveyed a joyful spirit of coming home at last in the presence of a loving and accepting father.

The painting affected me deeply. Without warning I felt tears coming fast and possibly some sobs. To get my emotions under control, I quickly moved away and stood apart from the gathering. As the group moved on I remained by the painting.

It was some time before I was able to rejoin the others.

My nephew Mark Hricko, also a Lutheran pastor, knew how much the story of the prodigal son meant to me. Sometime after my visit to Russia, he gifted me with a large reproduction of Rembrandt's painting. It now hangs over my desk as a reminder of the God who ever seeks us and loves us without end.

Over the years I've attempted to more fully comprehend why the story has had such a deep and moving effect on me. I've determined that it represents something more than a beautiful story. It touches the depths of my soul and leads me into the mystery of God's universe and, indeed, the nature of the Living Word.

I close this chapter as I began it, with the belief that Jesus' parable of the man and his two sons was his favorite story. If we knew no other stories except this one, I believe we'd know all we need to know of God and his loving nature. Also, it gives us power through his gracious love to redefine who we are and whose creatures we are. It shows us how to live a life seeking to become an embodiment of his love and spirit.

CHAPTER 3
DROPPING THE BONE

D avid Wilkerson, in his book, *The Cross and the Switchblade*, tells a story about his Pentecostal grandfather. The grandfather, a preacher, claimed that you don't take a bone from a bulldog without risking your hands. Rather, if you want to get that bone nice and easy, you just drop a big, juicy steak in front of that ol' dog. He'll drop that bone in no time flat.

The two parables in this chapter suggest something similar. They tell us that we sometimes need to give up the old to receive something new and better. Jesus tells one story about discovering a treasure in a field and another about finding a pearl of great price.

Here is the first of the two parables which appear in the 13th chapter of Matthew:

The Kingdom of Heaven is like a treasure hidden in the field, which a man found, and hid. In his joy, he goes and sells all that he has, and buys that field.

The second is the parable of the pearl:

Again, the Kingdom of God is like a merchant in search of fine pearls, who finding one pearl of great value, went and sold everything and bought it.

I believe these two stories are basic to entering the kingdom. The invitation to enter is always open to all of us, but there is a condition. In order to enter the heart and essence of the kingdom it is necessary to let go of anything that may become a roadblock or impediment.

The roadblock or impediment may be very different from person to person. One may be unwilling to let go of a grudge, a habit, self-righteous anger, or some prejudice he or she clings to. Another impediment may be the way we see others— poor, rich, racially different, sexually divergent—and thus refuse to love and accept them as God's children.

For many, the "condition" is too onerous and they turn their backs on the kingdom. A rich young ruler came to Jesus with the request, "What must I do to inherit eternal life?" Jesus knew that the young man had one hang-up, and that was his wealth. Jesus said to him, "Go and sell all you have and give it to the poor." This was the impediment for the young man. He was truly a good person but he couldn't part with his way of life.

It's been said that what you think about most of the time is what you become. A journey into our deep self not only gives us insight into our observable self but also into our shadow side. The shadow side and the subconscious are important in the discipline of self-discovery. We need to know ourselves. The more we know, the more complete we become, thus progressing toward the objective of the wholeness our Maker desires for us. The more we are able to listen to ourselves and to see ourselves, the more we can turn away from the ungodly, the hurtful, and a life that is less than complete. The prodigal son "came to himself." He rejected his current life and chose to go home. Each day is a day of turning—turning away from the thoughts and actions of the old self.

It is for us to dig into our conscious and subconscious minds to seek out that which may be a roadblock in receiving entrance into the new life of the kingdom. Hopefully, the insight and the vision of the kingdom will help to overcome the roadblock or impediment. It is the "steak" of life.

Jesus makes it clear that whatever you hold onto as a safety net must be let loose. You can't have it both ways. "Go and sell all that you have..." The kingdom must be the focal point; then all else falls into place. It's not a sin to be rich or powerful, but if wealth and power impede your making the right choices in life, the experience of the life-giving kingdom may be missed. The rich young ruler walked away rather than give up that which was blocking his entrance into the kingdom.

His predicament is similar to the illustrations in the following stories.

A zookeeper wanted to capture some chimpanzees for his zoo. After some experimentation he realized that they were wounding the animals in trying to capture them. He devised a plan. He emptied a large gourd and cut a hole in the side just big enough for the chimp's hand to reach inside the gourd. He filled the gourd with nuts and fastened it to a tree in the chimpanzee's path. When the chimp reached in and grabbed a handful of nuts, he could not get his hand out. The chimp had only to let go of the nuts in order to be free, but it would not. Thus it was captured and taken to the zoo.

A second story has to do with a man who slipped and fell over the side of a deep embankment. As he tumbled down to his death, he was able to grab hold of a small shrub and hold on for dear life. In his desperation he cried out, "God, help me!" After a moment he heard a voice say, "I hear you, my son, and I will help you. Just let go the shrub." There was a significant pause and then the man called out, "Is there anyone else up there?"

In his stories Jesus informs us that the men he described recognized the treasure—or kingdom—as something of great value. We may miss the value of the treasure. We may not be willing to take the risk of letting go of our fixations or our neurotic needs in order to gain entrance into the kingdom. Like the chimp, we cling to them. When the treasure is recognized for what it is, there is no contest. The steak beats the bone every time.

This chapter must end on the essential point of these parables. Jesus told his listeners that the kingdom of God is within. Each of us must seek it in the depths of our lives. It is here that we discover the heart of God and learn to know ourselves as precious and loved unconditionally. This is the heart of God's kingdom.

CHAPTER 4

LET GRATITUDE BE YOUR ATTITUDE

Some years ago I gifted members of my family with a plaque which read:

> Thou hast given
> So much to us
> Give one thing more--
> A grateful heart.

The foundation for creative and free living is to live in a state of gratitude. Gratitude comes when we know ourselves to be loved unconditionally. Gratitude is the natural response. Life thus becomes sacramental, an interior grace with an exterior manifestation. The command to love is not a legalistic demand. Once again, there is no requirement to obey the commandments in order to receive God's unconditional love.

Kingdom living is spirit-filled living. It is filled to overflowing. The overflowing is caused by having been given the most precious gift, the gift of love, of living free from restrictive laws or commands. Yet once we begin to live in a love relationship we overflow by fulfilling the commands and delighting in obedience to the will of God in Christ, to love one another. In one of the prayers of the Lutheran Church there is a passage in which I always found a significant affirmation. It reads: "... forgive us, renew us, and lead us so that we delight in your will and walk in your ways, to the glory of your holy name."

Delight is the word that should describe our obedience to love, serve and seek out the will and way of the Jesus. Commandments help us in times of confusion or doubt; they are the safety net we use in time of uncertainty. When Jesus said, "Take up my yoke upon you...it is easy," I believe he was not speaking of the burden of obedience to the law but rather a response of discipline and delight that is rooted in the attitude of gratitude.

There was a poster many years ago of a boy carrying his brother. The caption was, "He's not heavy, he's my brother." The yoke is not a burden, though it be heavy indeed, because of the joy and gratitude generated in the gift of love. It is a love that is as strong—and even mighty—as the challenge demands.

To recognize that God is indeed the giver of every good and perfect gift gives proper perspective. It helps us see that he is the very ground of our being, that he is the provider in all things. Even in sad and tragic situations he makes provision.

In Dostoevsky's book, *Crime and Punishment,* there is an unforgettable illustration of this in the person of Sonia. She supports her drunken father, her somewhat insane brother, and two other siblings. She is taunted by a friend regarding her circumstances and her faith. The friend criticizes her working as a prostitute to support her loved ones. He says, "...and where is this God of yours? What does he do for you?" Sonia's response is born of the deepest and most profound gratitude. She replies, "He does everything."

We recognize the difference between the gift that is freely given and the one that comes with strings attached. One gift is given by a grateful heart and one is given to serve personal aggrandizement. Over the years I've heard variations on the theme, "I'll never give him anything again. He doesn't deserve it." Or, "He never appreciates what I do for him." Some of the most committed church members are unkind in their conditional giving. How sad to miss the new heart of gratitude and remain stuck in the mire of legalistic exclusion.

Kingdom living is gracious. It is not founded on some principle or notion. It is always born of love unconditional. St. Paul identifies those who would be of the kingdom of God as new creatures, with the sweet smell of the Lord.

We are meant to be sweet smelling as followers of our Lord. He was. Read what Carl Sandburg wrote of him:

This Jesus was good to look at, smelled good, listened good. He threw out something fresh and beautiful from the skin of his body and the touch of his hands wherever he passed along.

The attitude of gratitude should be the music others perceive in the way we live. How often we hear only restrictions and judgments. Love and gratitude should be the music that we dance to as we share the good news.

⚔ ⚔

I close this chapter with a prayer given to me by a dear friend.

Every day of your life is a gift from God. Don't squander it. Don't waste it by being angry with anyone. Don't let it slip away by feeling sorry for yourself. Be grateful for this precious gift of life and spend it by being as happy and as thankful as you possibly can. Let your mind dwell on the good things which have happened to you. "Let gratitude by your attitude." Think of your assets and don't let anyone else spoil your day. Enjoy every day of your life to the fullest. Realize that you can add to the joy of each day by making someone happy. The kind of prayer that helps you get into the peaceful, grateful attitude might be something like this:

Heavenly Father, help me to be grateful for being alive right now. Help me to realize that no matter what problems there may be, where there is life there is hope. Help me to think positively and to realize that if I get my mind occupied by helping and cheering up others, I will be healthier than if I were always checking my own pulse. Help me to look for the good in everyone I meet. Let me realize that I can't change anybody's way of thinking. Only by doing the best I can and setting a good example may I influence someone to change their behavior. Help me to understand that other people have as much a right to their opinions as I do mine. Let me love myself as I am. Make me realize when I am not proud of myself that I am letting you, my creator, down. I must be proud of the body you have given me and realize there is a purpose for every person being different. Let me realize that you, my Father, are with me always, to guide and comfort me. Let me open my heart and my pores and let your love flow in. Let me accept the peace that you can bring; help me to understand that you have a plan and purpose for everything that happens. Amen

CHAPTER 5
UNUTTERABLE AND ECSTATIC JOY

"Unutterable and ecstatic joy" are the words Loren Eisely, in his book, *The Immense Journey,* used to describe two sparrow hawks being reunited. Eisely had been asked to capture some wildlife for a zoo while on an anthropological expedition. Here are his words describing the event as he held the limp body of a hawk he had caught in his net:

"He lay limp in my grasp and I could feel his heart pound under the feathers but he only looked beyond me and up.... I suppose I must have had an idea then of what I was going to do, but I never let it come up into consciousness. I just reached over and laid the hawk on the grass.

"He lay there a long minute without hope, unmoving, his eyes still fixed on that blue vault above him. It must have been that he was already so far away in heart that he never felt the release from my hand. He never even stood. He just lay with his breast against the grass.

"In the next second after that long minute he was gone... straight into that towering emptiness of light and crystal that my eyes could scarcely bear to penetrate. For another long moment there was silence. I could not see him. The light was too intense. Then from far up somewhere a cry came ringing down.

"It was not the cry of the hawk I had captured; for, by shifting my position against the sun, I was now seeing further up. Straight out of the sun's eye, where she must have been soaring restlessly above us for untold hours, hurtled his mate. And from far up, ringing from peak to peak of the summits over us, came a cry of such unutterable and ecstatic joy that it sounds down across the years and tingles among the cups on my quiet breakfast table."

As I read the account of Eisely's experience, I was caught up with his descriptive words and I resonated to them. "Unutterable and ecstatic joy": His words touch the deepest parts of our being. His words well describe loving and being loved. His words brim over with unutterable and ecstatic joy and goodness.

Joy is the word that Jesus uses in his stories to describe what it's like to discover that God loves us unconditionally and accepts us as we are. He uses the word in several parables. When the man found the treasure in the field and knew what it was, he went with joy and sold all he had in order to purchase it. When the prodigal arrived home, the father, in his joy, threw a party to celebrate his return. The woman who found her lost coin invited friends and neighbors to join with her in her joy. We sing, "Joy to the World," and the anthems resound with "Joy, joy, joy."

"Joy" is at the heart of the good news and the kingdom of God. Over the years, it's been helpful to me to differentiate between the words "joy" and "happiness." For the most part we use these words interchangeably, but they are significantly different. The word happy comes from a Nordic word meaning chance. It is filled with "ifs." "I'll be happy... if I pass the exam...if she goes out with me...if I get the job...if I win the lottery..." The list goes on and on. Happiness is thus conditional.

Joy, on the other hand, is constant. It comes through recognizing the gifts of life and that life is a gift. Joy has a sacramental quality. Joy is an interior state, a knowledge that we are unconditionally loved, which then makes itself known outwardly. We can be a person of joy even when things don't go our way. We find examples of unbounded joy in both literature and in real life.

In *The Christmas Carol*, Scrooge had been visited by three spirits and had come to himself. He was delighted upon discovering that he had not missed Christmas.

We see him at the window calling down to the boy in the street to confirm his hope that he had not missed Christmas. Then his joy overflows; his heart is filled with appreciation and good will. We witness his exuberant joy: He dances, he laughs, he sings, and his life is changed.

Then, too, there is the wonderful scene in *The Miracle Worker*, the story of Helen Keller. Blind and deaf from early childhood, the little girl was isolated from the world. The day came when Ann Sullivan, her teacher, finally got through to her pupil. As Ann pumped water into Helen's hand, she also spelled the word for water on the other hand. Suddenly the insight came to Helen. She made the connection. She wanted to know the word for everything; she ran around with joy and delight, having been set free.

Unconditional love is always a gift. Once it is discovered, it brings freedom from the captivity of needing to be happy. Joy is not something we seek, nor can it be manufactured. It comes as the by-product of good news. The words "I love you" bring the state of joy, fulfilling as they do, our need for loving, caring relationships. The Christmas carol, "Joy to the World" tells us that the good news of God's love, shown in Jesus, is the bringer of joy.

It is for us to contemplate the gift of joy and the way it enters our lives. The love of parents, husband and wife, children, grandchildren, friends and countless others who love and care for us are the bringers of joy. The greatest, however, is to know that the eternal lover is the ultimate bringer of joy.

Joy is the gift that overflows and becomes visible. It touches others with its power to transform and creates a chain reaction. It possesses an infectious and lasting quality, as evidenced by Loren Eisley's story of the sparrow hawks. Years later he could still feel the "unutterable and ecstatic joy" he experienced that day.

CHAPTER 6

HARD-WIRED FOR GOD

Over my desk hangs another plaque with the words of St. Augustine. It reads,

> Thou hast created us for thyself and our
> hearts are restless until we find our rest
> in thee, o Lord.

"Hard wired for God" might be another way of saying what St. Augustine meant. The thought that we are made for a relationship with the Eternal is staggering. It implies that in some way a homing device has been placed into us and that we are restless until we find our home in a relationship with God.

To those human beings who have the luxury to ponder such things, this question is of central importance.

They are caught up in the notion that the source of life is not only identifiable but that a relationship with the Eternal is possible, that it is to be recognized and appreciated.

Some people assume that knowing God is an impossibility, while others feel that it is more important to simply live their lives as decent people. For those who acknowledge God not only as a force or a being but one that we can relate to, however, it becomes the most significant of all relationships. In simple language, if God is the creator and if he created humans, God must be a personal God. As I stated previously, a staggering thought. On a bright, starry night, to contemplate the vastness and grandeur of the heavens and to think of God over and above it all, and then to contemplate that the kingdom of God is within you, that must be the most astonishing concept in all of human language and experience! It's too much for our limited intellect to conceive. We come to it through faith.

For the community that comes together as the kingdom of God, there is the belief that the person Jesus came among us as a human being and spoke of the Eternal God in a language that we could understand. It is believed that in him the mysteries of the universe were revealed. Through this historical person we are able to know God.

Being hard-wired for God, or having a homing device within, suggests that we are drawn to the spirit of this person of history. As we find the direction through Jesus, it is in our nature to seek "home." The two parables of this chapter reveal to us that the Eternal God seeks a relationship with his human creation; and, secondly, that at the same time, his human family seeks to be in a relationship with God.

Read the two stories that Jesus told. They appear in in Luke 15: 1-24.

Now, all the tax collectors and sinners were coming to listen to him, and the Pharisees and the scribes were grumbling and saying, "This fellow welcomes sinners and eats with them."

So he told them this parable: "Which one of you, having a hundred sheep and losing one of them, does not leave the ninety-nine in the wilderness and go after the one that is lost until he finds it? When he has found it, he lays it on his shoulders and rejoices. And when he comes home, he calls together his friends and neighbors, saying to them, 'Rejoice with me, for I have found my sheep that was lost.' Just so, I tell you, there will be more joy in heaven over one sinner who repents than over ninety-nine righteous people who need no repentance.

"Or what woman, having ten silver coins, if she loses one of them, does not light a lamp, sweep the house, and search carefully until she finds it. When she has found it, she calls together her friends and neighbors, saying, 'Rejoice with me, for I have found the coin that

*I had lost.' Just so, I tell you, there is joy in the presence
of the angels of God over one sinner who repents."*

Being lost can be as simple as getting mixed up in a
strange city; or it can be missing the point of what life
is all about, thus wasting the gift of life. Few things are
worse than being lost or being isolated from others.

The story of the lost sheep tells us that one sheep,
out of the hundred, somehow wandered off from the
flock. Maybe it was distracted, maybe it wasn't paying attention, or maybe it just wasn't very smart. Whatever the
reason, it was lost. The point of the story is that the shepherd knew that that one sheep was missing and went
searching for it, leaving the ninety-nine that were safe.
Scripture tells us that the sheep knew the shepherd's
voice and that he knew them. Jesus is clear that God,
the good shepherd, knows his sheep, and in turn, they
know his voice.

The second parable told of a woman who lost one
of her ten silver coins. She searched diligently until she
found it. The heart of this parable is, again, the per-
sistent searching for the lost. In these stories there was
great joy and celebration upon the finding of that which
was lost. Indeed, neighbors were called over to the house
for a party.

The two parables thus suggest that God seeks us and
that we, mortal creatures, seek God. I point to two other passages of scripture to support the first affirmation

that God seeks us. They are "...the kingdom is within..." and "...you are created in the image of God." There are many more.

The first, the "kingdom within," tells us that we discover God's unconditional love in the deepest part of ourselves. This would suggest that God is not to be found or experienced in the superficial—through ritual, creeds, or rote prayer. When we make the journey inward we not only discover our maker but also ourselves.

The second declares that we are created in the image of God, not in appearance, of course, but in a like nature, with a capacity for love and acceptance. Being created by God, we find it natural and easy to believe that we are of him. Having the marks of God, we are able to manifest the characteristics of the Eternal: To love unconditionally, to show compassion, to show mercy and forgiveness.

When we lose our way in our human journey, we become estranged or distanced from our God and lose our identity. The prodigal "came to himself" when he remembered his true home.

As creatures of our creator, we seek to reconnect with him, as our creator seeks to connect with us. It is a natural instinct, a homing device. We seek our wholeness, our unity, our at-oneness. We are restless until this happens. When we lose our way, we also lose our true selves. We become unloving. We lose mercy and compassion. Losing our identity puts us into estrangement with our true selves and allows us to become captive to sin, a word that means separation from God—a separation from good.

The result of this separation is the world we now experience. Where a world was created for harmony and unity, there is discord. Separation gives vent to the ugly, the hurtful, the greed-filled life. War breaks out between individuals, sects and nations. Peace of any lasting sort needs to be based upon the ultimate truth: unconditional love.

Being created in the image of God means that we are capable of loving unconditionally. Once again the parable of the prodigal comes to mind. As the son sought the father, so did the father seek his son. We are empowered to love like his father loved. We are called out to be perfect even as our heavenly father is perfect. Here, "perfect" is a process of becoming. The word perfect means "brought to completion" or being brought to "an end state." We may thereby assume that the journey of faith is a journey of growth. As we grow in love and compassion, we also grow in the image of God.

Hard-wired for God, or restless for God, thus states that we need to know that God is personal and is an abiding presence. There is a story about a father and son who have just returned from an exhausting day following the funeral of the wife and mother. There is not much conversation as both the father and son are caught up in their own thoughts and emotions. Finally the father tucks his little boy into bed and they both settle down to sleep. Not long afterwards, the boy appears at his father's bedside. He asks, "Daddy, can I sleep with you?"

He was welcomed and the lights were again turned off. For the longest time there was silence between them, until the little boy asked, "Daddy, is your face turned toward mine?" Lovingly, the father gave his young son the assurance that his face was, indeed, turned toward him; and, with this knowledge, the child was able to drift off to sleep. Even in the darkness that comes in this life, the knowledge that the Father's face is turned toward us has the power to bring comfort, rest, and peace.

When my own son David was six or seven years old, he came to my office in the lower level of our house. I said, "Hi, David, what's up?"

He responded with, "Oh, nothing." He didn't say anything but just stayed nearby.

I finally turned to him and asked, "Are you sure everything is okay? Do you need anything?"

His response, which delights me to this day, was, "No, I just like hanging out with you."

There are no more precious words that a father could hear. Jesus taught his followers to call God "Abba," which translates to "Daddy" in our language. It's a term of intimacy and caring tenderness. The full nature of God is a holy mystery, yet we as humans are to address the eternal God as Daddy!

John Steinbeck wrote, "A writer out of loneliness is trying to communicate like a distant star sending a signal. He isn't telling or teaching or ordering. Rather, he seeks to establish a relationship of meaning, of feeling, of observing. We are lonesome animals. We spend our lives trying to be less lonesome..."

Erick Fromm writes this in his book, *The Art of Loving*: "Unconditional love corresponds to one of the deepest longings, not only of the child but of every human being; but on the other hand, to be loved because of one's merit, because one deserves it...always leaves doubt; maybe I did not please the person whom I want to love me. Maybe this or that—there is always a fear that love could disappear. Furthermore, 'deserved' love easily leaves a bitter feeling that one is not loved for oneself, that one is loved only because one pleases, that one is, in the last analysis, not loved at all, but used..."

As strange as it may seem, I have discovered even in those who seem to be the most negative and uncaring a hope and desire for intimacy with "Abba." It is built into our human nature and we are indeed "restless until we find our rest in Thee, O Lord." We need to be loved on the highest level. The lack of it can create an ache of loneliness. I remember a very simple illustration of this that happened to me at age nine. The neighborhood kids were playing a game of hide-and-go-seek. Someone was "it" and everyone else went off to hide until the person who was "it" found us. In the game that day, I found the perfect hiding place under the steps of our front porch. I felt very pleased with myself until I realized that the voices of the kids got quieter. The noise of the group diminished and finally ceased altogether. I must have crouched under the steps for fifteen or twenty minutes. Finally the reality dawned on me that no one was looking for me! The game had moved on and I was not missed. That was over seventy years ago and I still remember it as if it were yesterday.

At the very heart of our lives is a need to be found and loved. As good as life may be without the love of God, a gap still remains when it is not present.

I close this chapter with a quote from 1st John 4: 11-14 and 16:

> *If God loved us so much, we too should love each other. No one has ever seen God, but as long as we love each other, God remains in us and his love comes to its perfection in us. This is the proof that we remain in him and he in us, that he has given us a share in his spirit. God is love and whoever remains in love remains in God and God in him.*

CHAPTER 7
HE REFUSED TO GO IN

If the story of the prodigal had ended with the party celebrating the return of the wayward son, it would have ended happily. But it didn't. Jesus added the elder brother to the story. The elder brother was unhappy when he discovered that his brother was home and a party was being thrown to welcome him. He refused to go in to join the celebration.

Read the ending of this story as Jesus told it. It appears in the 15th chapter of Luke's gospel.

Now, his elder brother was in the field; and when he came and approached the house he heard music and dancing. He called one of the slaves and asked what was going on. The slave replied, "Your brother has come, and your father has killed the fatted calf, because he has got him back safe and sound." Then the elder son became angry and refused to go in. His father came out and began to plead with him. But he answered his father, "Listen. For all these years I have been working like a slave for you, and I have never disobeyed your command; yet you have never given me even a young goat so that I might celebrate with my friends. But when this son of yours came back, who has devoured your property with prostitutes, you killed the fatted calf for him." Then the father said to him, "Son, you are always with me, and all that is mine is yours. But we had to celebrate and rejoice, because this brother of yours was dead and has come to life; he was lost and has been found."

The picture that Jesus paints of the elder brother is not flattering. Prim, proper, hard-working, he never gave his parents anything to worry about. Yet his character was fatally flawed: He was judgmental and unloving. While he did stay home and work on the farm, he did the right things for the wrong reasons. The great love passage from Paul's letter to the Corinthians describes the elder son well.

If I have all faith, so as to move mountains, but do not have love, I am nothing. If I give away all my possessions, and if I hand over my body to be burned, but have not love, I have gained nothing.

The elder brother was driven in his life style. He was known for his hard work and dedication to principle but he was judgmental toward others when they went astray. Although principled, he did not act out of love. He lacked love, kindness and forgiveness.

The younger brother was also driven. His was the drive of adventure, the good life, "wine, women and song." He was the opposite of his elder brother. He was irresponsible. In the end, however, "he came to himself," and went back home, while the elder brother did not "come to himself," and refused to go in.

Jesus taught that it was not the correctness of the law, or right thinking about the doctrines that counted; nor was it "doing good" by the letter of the law, or "dotting every i and crossing every t." Rather it was the law of love, according to the new paradigm, the new heart and mind.

The father left the party for his younger son and went out to encourage the elder son to come in and join the celebration. We have to believe that if the elder brother refused, the father would not give up trying. I'm bold enough to say that no one is ever excluded from the kingdom of God; exclusion comes about through an individual's refusal to go in or unwillingness to change. The only exclusion, then, is when we say, "No, I don't like the way they operate in the kingdom." This suggests that "I differ with the king, and I'm going to go my own way."

Jesus does not disclose the fate of the elder brother. Did he remain separated from his father and brother or did he "come to himself" as his brother did? Did he go home to become part of the kingdom of God?

Some time ago an article appeared in the *Christian Century* magazine. It told about an entire congregation being dropped from the rolls of a small denomination. The reason cited was that the congregation had taken a gay person into its membership. Like the elder brother, the denomination stood on its "principles."

Every bit as disturbing and sad was an episode on *Front Line* some years ago. A couple was being interviewed about their Lesbian daughter. She was asked to leave home because she refused to change her ways. The parents were asked by the interviewer: "If she called and desperately needed to come home, would you let her?"

The chilling response from this committed Christian family: "Not unless she changed."

Sin, as defined, is the separation from God. When we separate ourselves from others, or the church divides itself from others, a state of sin exists. We know that standing on principle can ofttimes be the wrong "stand." The kingdom of God—in this case, the Church--has all the gifts necessary to overcome division and adversity; but all the gifts are ignored when we insist upon being "right."

Daily life is filled with bigotry, sexual inequality, racial prejudice, and a multitude of hate-driven actions.

The self-righteous attitude is the attitude that Jesus sought to expose and change. Kingdom living, being one in Christ, strongly demands that we love one another and live in harmony. Indeed it is a divine imperative. God's Holy Spirit mandates that we cultivate an attitude of a non-judgmental openness to reconciliation and potential unity.

As members of the kingdom of God, we are called out to make love our law.

Nothing excludes us from the invitation to enter the kingdom of heaven except our refusal to accept the spirit of kingdom living. This parable of the elder brother teaches us that we have the choice to exclude ourselves from the kingdom. Yet the invitation is perpetually proffered. The father will continue to watch for the lost, be it the younger or the elder son, but he does not force either son to remain at home.

CHAPTER 8
LEFT BEHIND

A few years ago there was a series of books on the theme of "Left Behind." I read about three quarters of one of the books, more than enough to satisfy my curiosity. It was based on a familiar theme—one that can be seen on billboards along the highway, in front yards, and even on bumper stickers. The theme involves the end of life and poses such questions as "Will you be left behind at the second coming?" or "Are you prepared to die?" The fundamentalists who place such signs are prone to ask "Are you saved?" In doing so, they use threats to create anxiety and imply that without being saved, you will go to Hell.

Such believers base this threat, in part, on the parable of the ten maidens who were invited to provide a service at a wedding. In the time of Jesus, weddings were held at night. A procession formed at the home of the groom and paraded to the home of the bride. It was not unlike the marriage of my parents in Slovakia, when the procession from the groom's home included musicians and family as they made their way to the bride's home. In the days of Jesus, the procession was conducted at night, so it was necessary to have some light. This was provided by ten young maidens. Each carried a pole with a bowl on the top. In the bowl were some oil-soaked rags, which, when lighted, gave off a bright light.

Read the story as it appears in Matthew 25:1-13.

Then the dominion of heaven will be like this: Ten bridesmaids took their lamps and went to meet the bridegroom. Five of them were foolish, and five were wise. When the foolish took their lamps, they took no oil with them, but the wise took flasks of oil with their lamps. As the bridegroom was delayed, all the maidens became drowsy and slept. But at midnight there was a shout, "Look, here is the bridegroom. Come and meet him." Then all those bridesmaids got up and trimmed their lamps. The foolish said to the wise, "Give us some of your oil, for our lamps are going out." But the wise replied, "No, there will not be enough for you and for us. You had better go to the dealers and buy some for yourselves." And while they went to buy it, the bridegroom came, and those who were ready went with him into the wedding banquet; and the door was shut.

Later the other bridesmaids came also, saying, "Lord, Lord, open to us." But the bridegroom replied, "Truly I tell you, I do not know you. Keep awake therefore, for you know neither the day nor the hour."

The punchline in this story comes in the last sentence, "Keep awake therefore, for you know neither the day nor the hour." Jesus doesn't spell out the meaning of being awake, but more about that later. We do know that when the five foolish maidens arrived at the door, the answer was, "I don't recognize you so you are not permitted into the celebration." The five foolish maidens had gotten an invitation but it was tied to being part of the procession. They missed their calling and thereby missed the party.

Jesus called the five maidens foolish because they were not prepared. They didn't think ahead to the possibility that the groom might be late and that they might run out of oil. It is for us to interpret the meaning of this warning in our own lives and for our own time.

I believe it was not fear that Jesus sought to instill by telling this story. He didn't spend much time in condemning. He said, in fact, "I have not come to condemn the world but to save it." What did he mean, then, "to be prepared," or "to have enough oil?"

Without evaluating the number of possibilities, I suggest the one that most appeals to me. It is a call to experience the joy and celebration of life that we may

miss if we look elsewhere than the kingdom. The kingdom is not some distant event that we need to prepare
for, but the eternal now. Now is the time. We live in the
hour of abundant life.

We have all experienced being late for some en-
gagement or other. My wife and I attend the Maryland
Symphony and we quickly learned that once the perfor-
mance begins, late-comers are not permitted to enter.
Because they are asked to wait until the first musical of-
fering is completed, they miss some of the beautiful music. There must be a hundred illustrations as to why we
are late or why we put off getting prepared. We waited
too long to get ready. We were interrupted by someone
or something. Perhaps it was a last-minute phone call,
heavy traffic on the way, or not having good directions.

Jesus didn't describe the nature of the preparation
he had in mind. The church over the years has inter-
preted it in different ways, from the second coming of
Jesus to a warning of getting it right with God before it is
too late. There is indeed a warning in this parable. It
is not that you will be doomed to hell or separated from
the eternal. I believe Jesus is saying that it is possible to
"miss the wedding." I believe he means that it is possible
to miss out on the gift of joy and life offered in the ways
of the kingdom.

Jesus didn't seek to frighten those who heard him
with this warning. Rather he wanted to touch the deep
longing of his listeners. His news was exciting and

good. This is illustrated, for instance, in the parable of the man who discovers a treasure in a field and sells all he has to buy the field and possess the treasure. The good news introduces us to a God who holds the door open, who seeks the lost until he finds them. We are given the freedom and capability of making decisions for our life. Thus it is possible to make bad decisions, to be too late in taking advantage of the invitation to kingdom living.

Some forty years ago I met a man at a retreat. Let's call him Joe. As we shared together, Joe said he was a recovering alcoholic and had not had a drink in fifteen years. He was thankful for his life and freedom. He went on to relate that the greatest sorrow he had was for the twenty years he had lost because of his addiction. He said, "I lost my family, my job, and the life I could have lived. I missed out on being myself, on being a husband and father. I missed out on countless opportunities to simply live life. It was not God punishing me for my addiction; but until I received some loving care and support, I was left behind when it came to living the life that God entrusted to me."

Jesus points to a harsh reality. It's possible to get our priorities messed up. Jobs, making money, momentary pleasures—all of which may be good, but the kingdom needs to be first. Then everything else will follow. Jesus doesn't tell us what we need to do to prepare for the "celebration." It's left to us to figure out what he had in mind. I'll suggest some possible steps and leave others to your imagination.

First: Be awake to the amazing miracle of our existence and to the persons we are. In the parable of the prodigal there comes that phrase, "...and he came to himself." Jesus here suggests that, until this revelation, the young man was not himself. He was less a complete person and more what others made him. He lived a life but it was not his life. The first step, then, is to take the time to get in touch with who we are. The journey inward requires a dialogue with oneself about what is true and what is false. The journey is one of seeking to know ourselves, seeking to understand our motives and the power from without that would drive us to be something other than our true selves.

The second step is to include the Divine, our maker, God, in the journey inward. Here we need to listen to what has been communicated by God about his nature. There is the real possibility that, on our own and depending on our rationality, we would never discover his true nature. He revealed himself most dramatically in the person of Jesus; thus, in faith, we must learn to know the heart and mind of Jesus.

The next step leads us to know ourselves as children of God who are loved and accepted unconditionally.

The fourth step is the joyful living of the new and true self. Life becomes the sought-after joy. We learn to love and accept ourselves and thus we are able to love others. To me, this is the meaning of life.

Finally, we are more than rational creatures of God. In spite of the great gift of our rationality and all that it represents, we are more than logic or science. We are also persons gifted with the factor of faith. It is in faith that we receive our wholeness and wisdom. Science does give us wonderful information and does bring about newness, but does not impart meaning and purpose. It does not impart love.

No one is able to do the work of being awake and prepared for us. This is the work of the individual. The journey inward is not a walk in the park; it is, indeed, pursued with faith and trust. Making the journey gives us the promise of being awake and alive, truly alive to the amazing fact of our existence.

To be awake is to be in touch with the person we are and to know how we might best express our gratitude for life. To be awake is to know ourselves and then show our gratitude in loving others.

Some eight or ten years ago, I felt that the discipline of preparing for my death was in order. I gave myself two years for the task. My faith and trust were in place, but I was not sure that my emotional self was fully prepared. Within a matter of months, though, I gained the assurance I needed for the faith self and for my emotional self. The assurance for me was that, above all things,

I believed and trusted in the power of God's love. In some of my darkest days, I repeatedly wrote in my journal, "God will provide." In preparing for my death I was not convinced by an affirmation of faith, but rather by a life filled with God's abiding presence and provision. I saw the power of his provision in the life I lived. I simply added my death to the other experiences. God will provide in his perfect love.

Being prepared with the oil of life is then to store up the provision that God has granted. The power of God's presence is in the reality of days lived. There are many things that call for a faith commitment; but through much of the journey traveled, it is more than enough to live in joy and in hope.

The kingdom of heaven is a present reality. It is not some distant thing to fear. Yet to nurture and grow in the faith journey is a needful element. The door may indeed be closed because we are not prepared. Being "left behind" means missing out on the daily joys of living. The kingdom of heaven is to be seen as the zenith of priorities. It is the all in all. The invitation to be prepared is one of joy and not of anxiety. It is of critical importance that we do all within ourselves to daily grow in our preparedness—to live everyday aware of God's love and with faith in that love.

CHAPTER 9
USE IT OR LOSE IT

U se it or lose it. The phrase is familiar, whether it applies to mental power or muscle power. It is also the theme of the parable of investment. This parable has to do with the master of the household and his three servants. Read the story again. It appears in the Gospel of Matthew, chapter 25, verses 14 to 30.

For it is as if a man, going on a journey, summoned his slaves and entrusted his property to them; to one he gave five talents, to another two, to another one, to each according to his ability. Then he went away. The one who had received the five talents went off at once and traded with them, and made five more talents. In the same way, the one who had the two talents made two more talents. But the one who had received the one talent went off and dug a hole in the ground and hid his master's money.

After a long time the master of those slaves came and settled accounts with them. Then the one who had received the five talents came forward, bringing five more talents, saying, "Master, you handed over to me five talents; see, I have made five more talents." His master said to him, "Well done, good and trustworthy slave; you have been trustworthy in a few things, I will put you in charge of many things; enter into the joy of your master."

And the one with the two talents also came forward saying, "Master, you handed over to me two talents; see, I have made two more talents." His master said to him, "Well done, good and trustworthy slave; you have been a trustworthy slave; you have been trustworthy in a few things, I will put you in charge of many things; enter into the joy of your master."

Then the one who had received the one talent also came forward, saying, "Master, I knew that you were a harsh man, reaping where you did not sow, and gathering where you did not scatter seed; so I was afraid, and I went and hid your talent in the ground. Here you have what is yours."

But his master replied, "You wicked and lazy slave! You knew, did you, that I reap where I did not sow, and gather where I did not scatter? Then you ought to have invested my money with the bankers, and on my

return I would have received what was ?
interest. So he took the talent from him, a
the one with ten talents. For to all those who have, more
will be given, and they will have an abundance; but
from those who have nothing, even what they have will
be taken away. As for this worthless slave, throw him
into the outer darkness, where there will be weeping and
gnashing of teeth."

Most of us are more like the one talent man. It was
this servant, the one who had received the least to invest, who angered the master of the household. The
master had given to each according to "his ability." He
didn't expect the one-talent servant to accomplish what
the servants did who had two or five talents. What he
expected was that the one-talent servant would use what
he had. The master was furious and called the servant
who hid his talent in the ground lazy and even wicked.

Each of us has been gifted with the life we have.
We're not all expected to be great, but we are expected
to make the most of our abilities. It has been said that
on the day of accounting, God will not ask why were you
not Moses, Bach, or Einstein. Rather, the question will
be, "Why did you not use the abilities you were given?"

Many years ago I read a story in *The Reader's Digest*
about a woman who had a desire to build a greenhouse.
Years passed but she was never able to save enough money to have one built for her. Finally, one day in great

frustration, she decided to build it herself. Her friends said, "Impossible. You can't do it alone." She started, nevertheless. Using what money she had and scavenging the dumpsters, she constructed a greenhouse, bit by bit, all by herself. It was awful-looking, but it was a working greenhouse. She was delighted and joyful, and took great pride in her work.

The closing sentence in the story has stayed with me these many years. The woman concluded that "Anything worth doing is worth doing poorly." In effect, anything worth doing is simply worth doing! It doesn't mean that we set out to do a poor job; it means, rather, "Do the best you can with what you have."

I've enjoyed playing golf since I was a teen-ager. If I felt that I had to play like Tiger Woods or Arnie Palmer, I'd never have picked up a club. At the age of seventy-five I decided to learn to play the violin. If I felt that I had to play like Joshua Bell, I never would have started. Now, however poorly I play, I enjoy picking up my violin and playing a simple tune.

Opportunity beckons us with its possibilities. It is there with its fruit to be picked and enjoyed. Yet its season passes. "Carpe diem: Seize the day." In the story of the talents at the beginning of this chapter, Jesus cautions us loudly and clearly not to miss the opportunities presented to us.

The Romans pictured opportunity as a figure coming toward you, a person with a mop of hair on the front of his head, but bald in the back. If you meet opportunity face to face and recognize him, you can grasp him by the forelock and hold on to him; but if you let him pass you by, he is forever gone. There is no way of grasping an opportunity after it passes. There may be other opportunities in the future, but the past one is gone forever.

Life is filled with opportunities for us to use our talents, especially giving love and showing kindness. When we know about a person or friend in need, we often put off helping them, only to discover later that we are too late. We missed the chance to express our love or share our time with them.

In the story of the three men and the talents, the key words are opportunity, risk, and fear. An opportunity was presented, but, for the one-talent servant, the fear of the risk was too great. Fear is a major villain in our unresponsiveness to opportunity. The servant feared many things: He feared the master, who was a tough man; he feared failure; he feared losing the money he was to invest.

My mother loved to tell stories. One I'll never forget had to do with a young unmarried woman. The young woman, when asked why she never married, reasoned this way: "Well, if I had gotten married, I'm sure I'd be very happy. I would become pregnant and have a beautiful baby. One day my baby would be taking an afternoon nap and my husband would come home early from work. He would slam the front door, which would cause the picture over my baby's crib to fall and kill my child. So I'm never going to get married because I couldn't stand losing my baby."

Absurd? Of course. Yet how often the "what ifs" of life dominate our thinking and actions. As Martin Buber, the Jewish philosopher, said, "...if there were a devil, he would not be one who decided against God, but the one who, in eternity, came to no decision."

The story of the talents challenges each of us to joyfully spend ourselves. It is a story that says, "Go for it," or "Try it," or "You'll never know if you don't try." Our expectation is "each according to his ability," as the parable states. We are not expected to be a Tiger Woods or a Joshua Bell. What the parable expects from each person is to be our true best selves. Most of us are one-talent people, but we are promised that our ordinary self has the potential of becoming God's extraordinary creature.

Jesus writes his parables as earthly stories with eternal implications. Thus we learn from the stories wisdom for our journey in kingdom living. The talents parable cautions us about the opportunities we were too busy or too afraid to respond to--roads not traveled, the unspoken words of love and concern, the actions not taken, the needs not met—thus missing the reason for our being.

This story is an encouragement to live life fully and joyfully. Our lives are meant to be ones filled with giving ourselves away in love, as implied in kingdom living. God gives us our life to live, not to waste it or hide it in the ground. We must trust enough and risk enough. Jesus said blessed are those who share themselves and what they have with others. In other words, "use it" or lose the gift of experiencing the joy of God's gift of life.

CHAPTER 10
LIFE IS NOT FAIR

We've heard the words, we've uttered the words: "It's not fair." "His piece is bigger than mine." "He got the job because he had connections." "I was much more qualified." The list of "It's not fair" is a long one.

One story that Jesus loved to share is written in the Gospel of Matthew, chapter 20, verses 1-16. It tells of a landowner who needed workers and hired them from early morning until late afternoon. The workers were happy to have the work and worked hard. A problem arose, however, at the end of the day, when the workers were to be paid. Here is the story:

> *"For the kingdom of heaven is like a landowner who went out early in the morning to hire laborers for his vineyard.*

After agreeing with the laborers for the usual daily wage, he sent them into his vineyard. When he went out about nine o'clock, he saw others standing idle in the marketplace; and he said to them, 'You also go into the vineyard, and I will pay you whatever is right.' So they went. When he went out again about noon and about three o'clock, he did the same. And about five o'clock he went out and found others standing around; and he said to them, 'Why are you standing here idle all day?' They said to him, 'Because no one has hired us.' He said to them, 'You also go into the vineyard.' When evening came, the owner of the vineyard said to his manager, 'Call the laborers and give them their pay, beginning with the last and then going to the first.' When those hired about five o'clock came, each of them received the usual daily wage. Now when the first came, they thought they would receive more; but each of them also received the usual daily wage. And when they received it, they grumbled against the landowner, saying, 'These last worked only one hour and you have made them equal to us who have borne the burden of the day and the scorching heat.' But he replied to one of them, 'Friend, I am doing you no wrong; did you not agree with me for the usual daily wage? Take what belongs to you and go; I choose to give to this last the same as I give to you. Am I not allowed to do what I choose with what belongs to me? Or are you envious because I am generous'? So the last will be first, and the first will be last."

With a little imagination we can see the day: It was hot and humid. The laborers, anxious for work, appear at the entry to the vineyard before sunup and wait to be hired. They are delighted to have work at an acceptable daily rate. Others come, having heard that the vineyard owner was hiring. He hires all that come, until late afternoon. As darkness falls, they gather, the first to be hired and the last, all ready to collect their wage. Then the surprising thing happens. As the men begin to open their envelopes, they discover that everyone has been paid the same amount--those who were there at the crack of dawn and those who were hired late in the day. The grumbling begins. First they question whether or not there has been some mistake. The vineyard owner replies that there is no mistake. The grumbling turns to anger. "It's not fair! We worked all day through the awful heat and these others got here almost at quitting time. We deserve more!"

Then comes the punch line. "I promised you a fair wage and I gave it to you, right?"

"Yes, but it's not fair."

"Well, it may not be fair, but it's my money and that's what I want to do."

Here Jesus is presenting a new way of thinking and being. The story shows us a different style of life, a different God, a God who plays by different rules. For many of us, the rules of justice must be consistent. A person should get a just reward for services rendered and should be duly punished for a crime committed. For many, the balance of justice must obey the mandates of accepted principles. Jesus, however, sets all that aside in this parable. Under the rule of God there is a new standard, the bench mark is moved, and a very different scale is used.

The people who heard the parable were confused and conflicted. The sayings of Jesus seemed to contradict all they had learned about justice and fairness. The eternal law of an eye for an eye demanded compensation. The balance had to be set right. Here Jesus is changing the elemental rules that people had lived by. When Job was suffering through his afflictions, his comforters tried to convince him that he must have done some great wrong and thus was being punished. They believed that that was the way God acted.

Jesus changed that view and put forward a new vision. God was the all merciful, all caring, and unconditionally loving Creator God. Indeed, when Jesus suggested that God should be addressed as father, the word he used was "Abba," a most intimate of terms. Jesus states quite boldly that God is a loving God of inclusion. He plays no favorites among the workers in the vineyard but extends his grace equally to all, at whatever time they choose to accept it.

In spite of the protests, Jesus is saying, "That's the way it is in the kingdom of heaven." It is true that God does not play by man's rules of what is or is not fair. God is God, not a legalistic God, but one of compassion and unending love.

CHAPTER 11
I FORGIVE YOU

May God also Forgive You

I grew up in a family of rituals. My mother was creative in helping us celebrate and more deeply appreciate the holy days. One of the rituals I've been blessed and sustained by was that which took place before holy communion.

When I was about five years old (I remember because of where we lived at the time), Mother and Dad came to me shortly before I was to receive the sacrament.

"Daniel," they said, "if there is anything we have done to offend you, please forgive us." Then they taught me to respond, "I forgive you and may God also forgive you."

For a long time I believed the ritual originated in St. John's Slovak Lutheran Church in Johnstown,

Pennsylvania; but I later discovered it was, in fact, unique to my mother and our family. As years passed, it became a ritual that my sister Ann and I would follow, along with our parents, before communion. On my confirmation, it was my turn to seek out members of my family and ask their forgiveness. It was also necessary for me to visit with my godfather and repeat the words.

Over the years, communion, which had been administered four times a year in my church, became a monthly, and finally a weekly sacrament. Still, when we were together, we exchanged those words of forgiveness.

Most memorable for me was a time I was visiting my parents who, by then, were residents of the Lutheran Home in Johnstown. I arrived while they were at worship and sat between them. As it came time for the Eucharist to be administered, my dad reached across my chest and took my mother's hand. Their eyes met and, silently, the ritual was enacted again. It was and ever will be a precious moment in my memory.

The ritual has had a lasting effect on me. Seeking forgiveness and granting it is at the heart of life in faith. Early on I didn't understand it; but in time, I realized that the first step required of me was to seek peace through forgiving and forgiveness.

When Jesus told of unconditional love as in the story of the prodigal, he was also declaring that God was a God who understood our need to be loved and forgiven. The two go hand in hand: To love unconditionally also means unconditional acceptance and forgiveness. Read the words of Jesus regarding forgiveness as told in the parable of the king and his servant, from the 18th chapter of Matthew.

Then Peter came to Jesus and asked, "Lord, how many times shall I forgive my brother when he sins against me? Up to seven times?"

Jesus answered, "I tell you, not seven times, but seventy-seven times.

"Therefore, the kingdom of heaven is like a king who wanted to settle accounts with his servants. As he began the settlement, a man who owed him ten thousand talents was brought to him. Since he was not able to pay, the master ordered that he and his wife and his children and all that he had be sold to repay the debt.

"The servant fell on his knees before him. 'Be patient with me,' he begged, 'and I will pay back everything.' The king took pity on him, canceled his debt and let him go.

"But when that servant went out, he found one of his fellow servants who owed him a hundred denarii. He grabbed him and began to choke him. 'Pay back what you owe me,' he demanded.

"His fellow servant fell to his knees and begged him, 'Be patient with me and I will pay you back.'

"But he refused. Instead, he went off and had the man thrown into prison until he could pay the debt.

> *When the other servants saw what had happened, they were greatly distressed and went and told their master everything that had happened.*
>
> *"Then the master called the servant in. 'You wicked servant. I canceled all that debt of yours because you begged me to. Shouldn't you have had mercy on your fellow servant just as I had on you?' In anger his master turned him over to the jailer to be tortured, until he should pay back all he owed.*
>
> *"This is how my heavenly father will treat each of you unless you forgive your brother from your heart."*

The story ends with a stern word of warning. It states that if we have been loved and forgiven, it is also for us to love and forgive. Experiencing God's forgiveness is to have a heart that finds it imperative to also be forgiving. When we find it impossible to forgive, it's time to evaluate our lives, whether in the kingdom of God or the church. Anger and hurt have a way of clouding our spiritual vision, and we don't act according to God's holy spirit. An unforgiving spirit is a serious condition, serious enough to call forth harsh words from Jesus in this parable.

Our Lord's Prayer states, "Forgive us as we forgive." Forgiveness is central in the prayer of Jesus; it is vital to a living faith for kingdom living. Walter Wink tells of some peace workers who visited a group of Polish Christians after World War ll. They brought people from Germany who were seeking forgiveness. They desired a new beginning. As I remember the article, the Poles rejected their wish, saying that what was asked was impossible.

Before they ended their time together, the group prayed the Lord's Prayer. It changed everything. One of the Poles put it something like this: "If I did not agree to forgive you I could never repeat the Lord's Prayer again."

It is no small matter to be deeply hurt by another. The pain has a way of possessing us and gives us no peace; it threatens our well-being. No matter; we must find it in ourselves to forgive. If we find it impossible to let go of the hurt or to understand it in love, we need to pursue it until we are blessed with the insight needed to let it go.

Prayer can help us forgive. We might pray, "Help me in my healing. I know this is your will, but I can't do it by myself." It may help to envision Jesus with his arm around the person you can't forgive. "Yes Lord, I know those I hate are loved children; I'll pray for them and myself."

When the time is right, a call, a letter, or even a visit may be in order to begin breaking the wall of separation.

My favorite comic strip is Peanuts. Lucy is forever angry at Charlie for losing baseball games and isn't very forgiving about it. In one strip, Lucy is shouting at Charlie Brown, saying, "...and I don't care if I ever see you again. Do you hear me?"

With this she walks off and Linus says to Charlie Brown, "She really hurt your feelings, didn't she, Charlie Brown? I hope she didn't take the life out of you."

A sad looking Charlie Brown replies, "No, not completely...but you can number me among the walking wounded."

We can smile with Peanuts, but in fact, forgiveness in the giving and receiving is no laughing matter. To brood over wounds we have sustained from or inflicted on others can be debilitating, even for a lifetime. Each memory is like a whip that stings over and over. Such brooding takes away from our feeling of well-being.

There are those who are so unforgiving that they feel no qualms about writing off a son or daughter. They live by "principle" and "law," but not by the King's law of forgiveness.

I refer again to the disturbing interview I saw on *Frontline*. The situation involved the fundamentalist family whose Lesbian daughter was estranged. The parents were asked what it would take for them to accept her back into the family.

Interviewer: Do you miss your daughter?

Parents: No. We have no daughter.

Interviewer: If your daughter wanted to come home, would you accept her?

Parents: No, only if she changed.

I'm sorry that I have to write the conversation from memory. The actual interview was much sadder and more tragic.

Jesus had the greatest difficulty with people such as these, who had a narrow vision of the kingdom of God. One such group was the Pharisees. They were the watch dogs of precision; everything had to be precisely correct, according to the "law." Nevertheless, they missed what kingdom living was all about.

Healing and forgiveness are more difficult when we are apart from one another. To differ is part of human nature. "Different strokes for different folks." But division that ends in adversarial rejection must be seen as missing the point that is at the heart of Christianity: "That heart and that mind that was in Jesus." When there is contradiction, confusion, or lack of clarity in the church, we are, I believe, to seek to know that heart and mind of Jesus. It is safe ground; it is the ultimate solid rock. On the other hand, if we want to fight for our position, then we turn to church history, the creeds and the Bible.

Sin at its most destructive level is not about the sins of the flesh, but rather sins of the spirit-- being separated from God and others. Being estranged from ourselves and from God is thus at the heart of the matter in relation to forgiveness. It is easier for us to recognize our sins of the flesh than our sins of attitude. The elder brother refused to attend his brother's homecoming celebration. He was angry, pridefully angry. He was "right," and was not about to forgive his younger brother. He stood on principle.

The Psalmist of old had it right when he wrote in Psalm 51:10, "Create in me a clean heart, O God, and renew a right spirit within me."

It is for each of us to accept the unconditional love and forgiveness of God and to live a life in gratitude and forgiveness.

CHAPTER 12
THE PROCESS OF BECOMING

"We Are Not What We Shall Be"

Like being born, entering the kingdom is a new beginning. And with that beginning comes growth.
Growth is integral to life. It is also at the heart of being in the kingdom of God. We're fully human at our
conception and are always in the process of becoming.
Martin Luther put it magnificently when he said, "This
life, therefore, is not righteousness, but growth in righteousness; not health, but healing; not being, but becoming; not rest, but exercise. We are not yet what we
shall be but we are going toward it. The process is not
finished but it is ongoing—this is not the end, but it is

the road; all is not yet gleam and glory, but all is being purified."

The words of Luther bring comfort and strength. There are few thoughts that encourage me as much as "We are not yet what we shall be." We're a work in progress. Life is a growing, maturing, and fulfilling process. At times we feel about ourselves what the old Pennsylvania Dutch phrase suggests, "Too soon old, too late smart." But being on the way is exciting. It's gratifying to know that, whatever stage of life, we're in the groove and we're moving. The essential thing is to make sure we are on our way.

Consider how we plan for a flight. We may spend a good deal of time studying all the materials about the 747, the flight schedule or the seating chart. We may even go to the airport to check its layout. But the fact is that all this preparation doesn't move us an inch. Only when we board the aircraft and it takes off does the trip actually begin. Then we are moving. The old is left behind and the new gets closer.

Jesus told two parables about growth and its importance in the kingdom of God. They appear in the Gospel of Matthew, Chapter 13, verses 31-32, and in verse 33.

He put before them another parable: "The kingdom of heaven is like a mustard seed that someone took and sowed in his field; it is the smallest of all the seeds, but when it has grown it is the greatest of shrubs and becomes a tree, so that the birds of the air come and make nests in its branches."

He told them yet another parable: "The kingdom of God is like yeast that a woman took and mixed in with three measures of flour until all of it was leavened."

The people who followed Jesus understood the story of growth. They experienced growth in their daily lives. They saw their plants grow and produce. Daily they baked bread and knew the delightful end to the process.

We've all seen plants in the windows of elementary schools. The teacher helps the class to observe how things grow. A seed doesn't look very promising when it's planted; but the teacher explains that everything needed for life is contained inside that seed, except for water, which the students will provide. Almost daily the students see the process of growth unfold before their eyes as the tiny leaflets emerge from the soil and stretch toward the sun.

Yeast is every bit as dramatic as the growth of a seed. When added to flour and water, it has the power to transform. I once read that yeast is a fungus that consumes the sugar in the dough and creates gas as a by-product. The gas is trapped in little pockets throughout the dough. It expands slowly and quietly. Working from the inside, yeast is able to change the texture, the looks, and the taste of the dough. The bread would be flat without the yeast.

Jesus declares that growth is part of kingdom living. It is not something we can make happen. It is, instead, a natural happening once you enter the new realm. The growth may be invisible or dormant for long periods of time. That the tiny mustard seed could become something as large as a tree in which a bird might nest seems impossible; but in due time, the results are delightfully visible.

The secret in the kingdom of God is not unlike a seed or yeast. Both need to be cultivated and allowed to flourish. There is a period of planting, a period of growth, and, finally, there is a harvest. The planting has to do with the process of accepting the unconditional love of God; the second part of the process is that of living in the state of that love; and the third is living fully the life of being God's lover.

The Quaker Hannah Whittal Smith, in her book, *The Christian's Secret of a Happy Life*, wrote this: "We all know that growing is not a thing of effort, but of an inward life principle of growth. All the stretching and pulling in the world could not make a dead oak grow; but a live oak grows without stretching...the essential thing is to get within you the growing life...hid with Christ in God, the wonderful divine life of an indwelling Holy Ghost... Abide in the vine. Let the life from Him flow through all your spiritual veins."

I once saw a bumper sticker that read, "Be patient with me. I'm a work in progress." It's an exciting thought to know I'm not what I shall be. Instead, even in my eternal rest, I will continue to grow.

CHAPTER 13

THERE'S A HOLE IN THE BUCKET

Harry Belafonte popularized the song that has the same title as this chapter. The lyrics of the song convey the frustration of trying to fix a hole in the bucket. Each time Martha suggests a potential solution, Henry needs something more to fix it. There was no way to mend the hole in the bucket. The central truth of the song is that a fixed-up bucket would not do; they needed a new bucket.

Jesus presented two versions of this problem in Mark 2: 21-23.

First, "*No one sews a piece of unshrunk clothing on an old garment; if he does, the patch tears away from it, the new from the old, and a worse tear is made.*"

The second parable reads, "*And no one puts a new wine into old wineskins; if he does, the wine will burst the skins and the wine is lost, and so are the skins; but one puts new wine into new wineskins.*"

In these twin parables Jesus points out the danger of mixing the old and the new. The parables would be understood by those who heard the words of Jesus. They knew about a piece of new cloth being used to patch a hole in an old garment. It would shrink upon washing and end up tearing the garment. Likewise, people knew better than to put unfermented wine into old wineskins. The old wineskins would have become hard and cracked easily. The fermenting wine would put enough pressure on the old skin to cause a break and the loss of both wine and skin.

When Jesus speaks of the kingdom of heaven he makes it clear that the old and new do not mix. The kingdom of heaven is so different that it's not possible to patch the new onto the old way of thinking. The very essence of the new is so dramatic that it does violence to the old. The parables served as a response to the Pharisees who were critical of Jesus. They assumed that the combination of the old and new could be used together. Jesus opposed the Pharisees because they were stuck in the old and claimed rightness. They missed the heart and the very essence of the good news—the news of unconditional love.

It seems that in all of recorded history we find evidence that the old or conservative mentality is ever put forward as the standard to uphold. The new is rejected. Even today the church continues to divide because many are faithful to the wrong foundation. Their foundation is based on the "law" and not on unconditional love.

In the time of Jesus the people had been pro-grammed to live in the old way, to follow "tradition," as Tevya sang in *Fiddler on the Roof.* Their traditions came with a great deal of ritual laws and demands, demands that were often a burden to the common people. Yet they were the standard of the day, as put forth by the religious community. Jesus, in the New Testament, was calling for a new day, for a new heart, for kingdom living in unconditional love, and not simply following old and worn-out empty ritual.

The invitation to become kingdom dwellers does not simply seek to help us become better or improved but rather to enter into a new state. Thus, some things are impossible to combine. For example, it's not pos-sible to love unconditionally and yet believe in slavery. Many who called themselves Christian felt there was nothing wrong with owning another human being. Unconditional love and slavery don't mix. Indeed, the latter will destroy the other, so great is the contradiction.

In Jeremiah 31:33 and 34, Jesus gives evidence of the new way: *"This is the covenant I will make with the people of Israel after that time…I will put my law within them and write it on their hearts… No longer will they teach their neighbor, or say to one another, 'Know the LORD,' because they will all know me, from the least of them to the greatest... For I will for-give their iniquity and will remember their sins no more."*

Jesus was advocating a transformation into the un-conditional love of God and the knowledge of it first-hand, in a personal way, the new way. It is the difference between reading a book about love and being in love. The one provides information and correct attitudes, but the latter produces a spontaneity that comes from being a new person.

Jesus could not have been more dramatic in describ-ing the difference between God's kingdom and the old way of living by the old laws. He said that the newness was so different that it was like being born anew or born again. We are aware that being born a second time is not possible; Jesus was stating that to be born of the flesh and to be born of the spirit were two totally dif-ferent things. As he explained to Nicodemus, when you come to yourself, your true self, it's so different it's like being born again. The old passes away and everything is new: the way we perceive, the way we understand, the goals we set, our time, our energy, our very lives are set in motion to change.

Jesus had regard for the old but said that it needed to be brought to fulfillment. The meaning here is that it be brought into the new paradigm. The old is to be fulfilled by the new. A banner that hung over the en-try to the United Church of Christ at the Chautauqua Institute in New York State contained the words, "God is still speaking." In other words, God is not dead but continues to reveal the new to his people. For all too many Christians, the last word was said in scripture, in the Creeds, and through church history. They prove their stand on an issue by quoting from one or all of these. It appears to me that even unchristian stands can be upheld by quoting the Bible. The revelations are not that God changed but rather that humankind didn't get it earlier. Old things have passed away. Behold the old has become new.

There's a hole in the bucket and patching it won't do; a new bucket is required. Only the new creation of love will do in the sight of God—a word written on the heart.

CHAPTER 14
KEEP ON KEEPING ON

Jesus told two stories about persistence. We can hear him cheering us from the side lines: "Don't give up...Hang in there...Have hope...I'll be with you all the way..." Both stories must have brought a smile to his listeners. They knew situations and people just like those he described. Read the two stories as they appear in the Gospel of Luke. First, Luke 18, verses 2-5:

> "There was in the city a judge who had no fear of God and no respect for man. And there was a widow in that city, and she kept coming with a plea, 'Grant me justice against my adversary.' For some time he refused. But finally he said to himself, 'Even though I don't fear God or care about men, yet because this widow keeps

bothering me, I will see that she gets justice, so that she won't wear me out with her coming.'"

The second story has the same theme and encourages perseverance. It is written in the eleventh chapter, verses 5-15 in Luke's gospel.

And he said unto them, "Which of you shall have a friend, and shall go unto him at midnight, and say unto him, 'Friend, lend me three loaves; for a friend of mine in his journey has come to me and I have nothing to set before him'? And he from within shall say, 'Trouble me not. The door is now shut and my children are with me in bed. I cannot rise and give thee.'

"I say unto you, though he will not rise and give him, because he is his friend, yet because of his importunity, he will rise and give him as many as he needeth.

"And I say unto you, ask and it shall be given you; seek and ye shall find; knock and it shall be opened unto you.

"For everyone who asketh receiveth; and he that seeketh findeth; and to him that knocketh it shall be opened.

"If a son shall ask bread of any of you that is a father, will he give him a stone? Or if he ask for a fish, will he give him a serpent? Or if he shall ask for an egg will he offer him a scorpion?

"If ye then, being evil, know how to give good gifts unto your children, how much more shall the Heavenly Father give the Holy Spirit to them that ask him?"

In these two stories Jesus helps us understand the value of persistence and perseverance. We learn as we travel life's journey that "practice makes perfect," or at least it helps us grow. This is a well-known truth for many aspects of daily life. If we want to become good at something we need to persist.

Following my second retirement at the age of seventy-five, I fulfilled a life-long ambition to take violin lessons, where I was introduced to the Suzuki Method. I came across a phrase by Mr. Suzuki in some of his written materials that impressed me. He said, "Learn a piece of music, and then play it 10,000 times." I can't count the number of times I've played "Twinkle, Twinkle Little Star," but I still don't sound like Itzhak Perlman. I'll continue trying, nevertheless.

My son-in-law David Petrie was an "Iron Man" triathlete. I asked him what it takes to compete in such an event. High on his list of requirements was, "Don't give up. Stick with the discipline of getting in shape and staying in shape."

In some of the darkest days of World War II, Winston Churchill challenged the people of Great Britain with the words, "Never give up." These words of encouragement have been repeated by parents, teachers, coaches, trainers, and a host of others.

There is a story told by a Zen philosopher. It tells of a youth who wanted to increase his already considerable skill as a swordsman by studying the Zen art of swordsmanship. He apprenticed himself to an old Zen master swordsman who lived under Spartan conditions in a remote area of Japan. The young man agreed to cook and clean in return for instruction. Initially the young man did nothing but cook and clean. Finally, tired of the lack of action, he demanded that some sort of lessons begin.

"Next Monday," the old man replied.

On Monday the young man got up early as usual to start the fire. Suddenly the old man appeared out of nowhere and hit him a resounding blow across the shoulders with a stick. The young man was not so much hurt as startled and very puzzled. During the next months his life was made miserable by the constant assaults of the old master, who was ever more inventive in his ways of catching him with his guard down. If the youth was initially startled, he eventually became extremely tense and wary as the blows continued.

Finally he decided that the old man must be senile. He thought that the blows, which really did not hurt much, were an attempt to humiliate him. He became bored with the procedure, which went on and on. After much time, it became possible for him to fend off the attack. He simply reacted and parried the blows.

One morning the young man got up to make the rice and discovered the old man already awake and bending over the rice pot. He was holding the lid in one hand while stirring with the other. Over the old man's head lay the stick that had so often been used to strike the youth. He couldn't resist. Grasping the stick in a swordsman's hold, he swung directly at the old man's head. In the last split second, the old man flicked up the pot lid and parried the blow. In that instant the young man realized that his period of instruction was over.

The goal of persistence is that eventually the door will open, the desire will be fulfilled. The hope is that discipline will produce a response that comes naturally—a response that is part of our new state of being in the kingdom.

The poet Henry Wadsworth Longfellow wrote, "Perseverance is a great element of success. If you only knock long enough and loud enough at the gate, you are sure to wake up somebody."

The difficulty arises for many when a loved one is sick. We pray for the loved one but the prayer is not answered in the way we wish. We pray for bread, i.e. healing, but we get stone, i.e. death. Others pray to be relieved of pain, or to recover from a disaster, or to heal a bad relationship, all to no avail. This can be a discouraging time.

Nelson Mandela captures the spirit of this frustration when he writes: "I know that Qamata (God) is all-seeing and never sleeps, but I have a suspicion that Qamata may be in fact dozing. If this is the case, the sooner I die the better, because then I can meet him and shake him awake and tell him that the children of Ngubengcuka, the flower of the Xhosa nation, are dying."

Then there are those who say that God always answers prayer; we just don't understand his answer. For many, that is no answer at all. Others say that God is with us in all the circumstances of life, including the most profoundly sad times. It is not that God needs to be pestered in order to receive what we seek, but rather that the kingdom of God is within us and we need to continue the quest. Eventually an answer will be found.

Life challenges us on many fronts. At times it appears easier to throw in the towel, to give up, to quit. Still, the discipline of persistence gives abiding hope. It is contained in a phrase that Jesus said, "I am with you always." It is the abiding presence of our Maker and our Lord, through his unconditional love, that sustains us. With it, we are able to keep on keeping on.

CHAPTER 15
ACCENTUATE THE POSITIVE

Eliminate the Negative, and Don't Mess with Mr. In-between

The parable of this chapter is about a house. We might call it a haunted house. It was demon-possessed, a popular belief in the time of Jesus. In the story, Jesus is talking about the kingdom of God and the dangers in our spiritual journey. I believe Jesus is saying that there are demons in the house of the self. Read the words as they are written in the gospels of Matthew 12:43 and Luke 11:24.

> *When an unclean spirit comes out of a man, it goes through dry places looking for rest, but doesn't find any.*

Then it says, "I'll go back to the home I left." It comes and finds the house swept and decorated. Then it goes and takes home with it seven other spirits worse than itself, and they go in and live there. In the end, that man is worse than he was before.

Most people in our day don't make much of possession by spirits and demons. Yet it's not unusual to hear someone say, "He's plagued by demons," meaning that some bad habit or some sinful way possesses that person. Depending on the definition of demon, I believe it's fair to say that we all have our demons. We are less than perfect and thus our lives are not without some thoughts or actions that frustrate our wholeness.

The unclean spirit is a thief. Its role is to take away from the abundant life that God planned for his creation. The parable states that to clean out one bad or debilitating habit and to put nothing positive in its place may in fact make the last state of the house worse than the first. Allowing for the reentry of one evil or bad habit may truly weaken one's defense against others. A little cheating such as "Just one more..." or "Just this one time..." can be an entry for many additional evils potentially worse than the first.

A popular song in the 1940's was entitled, "Accentuate the Positive, Eliminate the Negative." The old song with the peppy tune captures the spirit of what Jesus is seeking to teach us. In this parable, he is saying that we need a new spirit—a new tenant in our house. We need to re-place the negative with something strong and positive. It has been said that nature abhors a vacuum; something always fills up the emptiness

"Accentuate the positive" is rife with possibilities. Books of spiritual discipline can help. The old writ-ers such as Thomas a'Kempis (my favorite during my college days) and more contemporary writers such as Richard Foster give spiritual direction. Easy reading, yet profoundly insightful, is the work of Henri Nouwen. Writers such as these can help us drive out the bad and make room for the good in our way of thinking.

The point of the parable of the haunted house is that you can't simply rid yourself of some evil or bad habit by stopping for a while. It's necessary to make a new commitment—a commitment that fills the empty space left by the evicted spirit with something good. This process involves three steps. The first step is to look deep within ourselves to identify any evil spirit that resides there. Second is the work of ridding ourselves of the evil; and finally, and most importantly, replacing the evicted evil with a positive arsenal of values and be-haviors that fortify our lives.

The first step is the journey into ourselves. Because of the unconditional love and accepting spirit of our maker, we are able to look ourselves in the eye and see ourselves as we really are without shame or guilt. This self-examination is essential. We see the loved person that we are, but also the warts, the shadow side, the dark places. Scripture gives us a platform on which to stand and observe our values: the heart and mind of Jesus. Great care needs to be given regarding our defensive posture that we not justify our values by our personal and selfish desires. For example, it's nearly impossible, as a follower of Jesus, to be against the poor and their needs. Jesus is clear in his affirmation on the subject. Prejudice has many faces and our spiritual houses need to be cleared of any of those faces that live within. A buzzword that gives us a hint that we may harbor negative thoughts and feelings toward others is when we refer to others as "they."

Our spiritual housecleaning requires us to meditate on our thoughts and feelings, and, upon discovering an evil spirit, to begin the second step, the work of eviction. All of us have ways of behaving that are less than positive. We say hurtful words and are critical, or we become defensive at the slightest criticism. Among the classical list of potential evil occupants in our houses are greed, lust, laziness, self-centeredness, self-righteousness, and an unloving or unforgiving spirit. Add your own to the list. The evil tenant is our enemy and would do us or those we love harm.

As Pogo says, "We have met the enemy and it is us." Through the inward journey, accompanied by the abiding presence of God, we become free enough and strong enough to then evict the hostile or harmful habits and unclean spirits. I like the idea of practicing. Repeating a new behavior is the best way to allow it to become entrenched. I've heard that a new behavior becomes ingrained by faithfully repeating the behavior daily for a month.

To evict a bad behavior, practice a new, more loving behavior in its place. Let's assume for a moment that a problem you are not happy with is your inability to listen well. The art of listening can be a learned skill. In the process you will need to shut down your internal urge to interject your own thoughts while listening to another. Practicing not only helps the new habit evict the old, it eventually makes the "new" become part of our nature—our natural response.

Keeping the new spirits within and the evil spirits out is an act of discipline. As members of the kingdom, we learn the way of Jesus and about kingdom living. Discipline includes filling our lives with loving, positive behaviors so that there is no room for the evil to invade and take over our lives. J.B. Philips, in his translation of the Epistles, tells us to "squeeze" out the evil with an overflowing love. This has to do with our thinking; the things we think about most of the time are what we are shaped by and become.

Accentuate the positive suggests filling our lives with positive actions in daily life. Becoming good lovers of mankind is at the heart of life in the kingdom, or, as members of Christ's body, life in the church. We learn to see and hear others in a positive light, and we seek to respond. It's not enough to be against some evil in the world around us. It is also necessary to be available and accountable, to be proactive in the cause of justice and benevolence. "As you have done it to one of the least of these, you have done it to me."

To be proactive may mean that we must move out of our comfort zone. If walls of comfort have been built in our lives—in our churches, our communities, our nation—it is for us to tear them down and evict the bad spirits: harboring prejudice; keeping the status quo at the expense of the poor and disenfranchised; advocating government programs that would take away assistance to the needy and disabled. We must continue to be positive and proactive when it comes to services Jesus would support: feeding the hungry, affirmative action, universal education and health care, to name a few. It should upset us when we read that the rich are getting richer and the poor are getting poorer. This is especially true when those who work daily to produce that which makes the rich even more prosperous don't themselves benefit from that labor.

Replace hate with love, replace anger with good will. Read a list of suggestions from Paul's letter to the Christians in Romans 12:9-17 and 21.

> *Let love be genuine; hate what is evil, hold fast to what is good; love one another with mutual affection; outdo*

one another in showing humor. Do not lag in zeal, be ardent in spirit, serve the Lord. Rejoice in hope, be patient in suffering, persevere in prayer. Contribute to the needs of the saints; extend hospitality to strangers.

Bless those who persecute you; bless and do not curse them. Rejoice with those who rejoice, weep with those who weep. Live in harmony with one another; do not be haughty, but associate with the lowly; do not claim to be wiser than you are. Do not repay anyone evil for evil, but take thought for what is noble in the sight of all... Do not be overcome by evil but overcome evil with good.

In other words, accentuate the positive, eliminate the negative, and don't mess with mister in-between.

CHAPTER 16

ARE YOU SOMEBODY?

Some years ago I was visiting Ocean City, New Jersey, with two dear friends. We stopped for some refreshment at the Point Pub. A golf tournament was being held in a nearby community which brought many professional golfers to the area. As we were being served, our waiter asked me, "Is he somebody?" nodding toward my friend Albert with the assumption that he might be one of the golfers. Our friend Barry, without missing a beat, answered, "No, he's nobody." We laughed.

I was reminded of a story about Michael Deaver who served as an advisor to President Reagan. While traveling on a plane he was asked, "Didn't you used to be someone?" I, too, once had a similar experience on a trip home to Johnstown, Pennsylvania. I stopped at a diner and during my time there my waiter asked me,

"Shouldn't I know you?" I couldn't resist saying, "No, I'm nobody."

The question, "Are you somebody," is a vital one. How we think of ourselves can determine how we act and see ourselves; it has the power to transform our inner world. Depending on how we think others see us also has the power to shape our perception of ourselves. The Scottish poet Robert Burns said, "O wad some Pow'r the giftie gie us, To see oursels as ithers see us!" Most important is the ability to see ourselves the way God sees us.

It has been demonstrated in clinical tests that we are bent by the opinion we have of ourselves. If we see ourselves as losers, we will carry this image into all facets of our daily lives. Jesus echoed the words of the Old Testament, saying, "As a man thinks, so he is." In Shakespeare's *Hamlet*, Hamlet says to Rosencrantz and Guildenstern, "For there is nothing either good or bad, but thinking makes it so." What we think may not represent the facts, but our perception makes it so.

We are created to be "somebody." Each of us is unique, created to be our true selves. The Prodigal Son found his true self when he "came to himself." He entered the world of salvation. When we enter the world of salvation, we become what God created us to be. We are not to be better than or different from; we are to be our true selves.

Remember that one definition for salvation is wholeness or completeness. Being loved by God, we are given the power to aspire to the image of God—not a physical image, but an image of love and compassion. Although we were created in his image, somehow we become, through our actions, less than God meant us to be. Because of the distortions that life brings, we lose our wholeness. We are less than perfect, less than loving. Like the Prodigal, we seek the "good life" through highly personal and subjective ways and become entangled in our search. The disentanglement is part of the process of God's bringing us back to the original image, our true self.

There are many reasons why we stray from our true self. I feel confident that it has nothing to do with God giving an indictment to all humankind because of the sin of Adam and Eve. This would hardly fit the God of love. The nature of our humanity is a mystery; but we do believe that God, in his love, has given us the freedom to become our true selves. The world around us has the power to mold us, to bend us out of our true shape. The world around us includes parents, relatives, friends, teachers and the multitudes of those who pass through our lives.

To be "born again," it is necessary to discover and confront ourselves, and to seek God's presence as we make the journey of self-discovery. Being "born again" or "coming to ourselves" may happen in an instant or gradually over time. Either way, it is of the utmost importance to learn to know in our deepest selves the love of our Maker and our Lord.

In order for us to know ourselves we need to delve into the heart of our very being. The journey inward is one that includes being in touch with our motivations, our actions, our thinking. It is a quest for the conscious and the subconscious self. It explores our fears, our anger, our frustrations—the dark shadowside of ourselves—as well as our joys and delights.

There is some puzzlement about what we are to seek first. Jesus said, "Repent and believe." At times I wonder if it is not necessary to believe first and then, in the context of unconditional love, change. Perhaps there is no one way; the individual will discover the way as he or she is seeking.

My hoped-for end result of the journey is that we see ourselves; we come to our true self. Then we are in touch with the eternal and learn of God's total and unchanging love. When we know ourselves to be loved fully and unconditionally, we recognize ourselves as children of God. It is then that we become "somebody." Becoming somebody by the grace and love of God, we then become sacramental people, i.e., people of God with the power to pass it on. "It only takes a spark to get the fire going." We become lovers of God. It is our calling and the reason for our living and our being. We learn to love and accept ourselves and we are then empowered to reach out and love all others. It is thus we are created in the "image of God."

I complete this chapter with several stories that demonstrate the power of the sacramental, that being an internal grace with an external manifestation. The power can come through individuals or groups. In the eternal spirit of the Christ, we become the hope of the world.

I'm sorry to say that I don't remember the sources of the first two stories. The first shows the power of the spirit of love transcending the simple rational. It's about a missionary who was sent to a remote part of Africa, a place he thought no one from the outside world had ever visited. After learning the language, the missionary began to teach the people about Jesus. As they listened, their faces brightened with excitement. They said, "We know him. He was here among us." Mystified, the missionary began to explore what they could possibly mean by this assertion. After some inquiry, the missionary discovered that he was not the first white person to visit the people in this remote village. Years before, there had been another missionary who had spent some time with the villagers. He never learned their language but worked among them and cared for them. He lived among them as the Christ-like man that he was. They never learned the name of Jesus, but they believed they knew him. His was a sacramental self.

The second wonderful story involves a monastery that had fallen on hard times. There were only a few monks remaining. People never visited as they once had. The abbot was troubled and went to visit his neighbor and friend, the Jewish rabbi. They sat and talked about the hard times. Finally it was time to go and the rabbi said to the abbot, "I have no advice to give you, but the one thing I know is that one of your members is the Christ."

All the way back to the monastery the abbot pondered the rabbi's parting words. "One of our brothers is the Christ," he thought over and over. When he returned to the monastery he shared the words of the rabbi with all the brothers. It caused a stir among them. Who could it be? Each began to consider which of the brothers might be the Christ. "Could it be Brother John? No, that's not possible because Brother John eats too much. On the other hand he is most considerate. Perhaps it is Brother John..." All the brothers contemplated each other and in each case the final thought was it could be any one of them.

As the weeks and months went by the atmosphere changed in the monastery. Everyone noticed it. Everyone was kinder, more considerate of every other monk. There was a more joyful spirit and not as much grumbling. Some of the monks began to sing as they worked, and they formed a small choir. They sang from the heart so beautifully that people began to come. They picnicked on the grounds and listened to the monks sing. They felt such joy, such love! The people felt uplifted. Then an amazing thing began to happen. Young men came to the monastery wanting to join the fellowship. Very soon the community was again thriving, and people said of the monastery, "See how they love each other."

My final story was told by Father Brennan Manning. I tell it from memory. Richie was a student at the University of Notre Dame. By any standard Richie was a slob. He was unkempt in appearance, overweight, had a lisp, and was not into bathing. He was easy to avoid and most of the other students did just that. The college chaplain's office was one place he frequented often. He was on the verge of failing and being dropped from the student body.

Christmas break came and Richie went home to spend it with his family in Boston. Father Manning stressed that Richie's parents were Irish Lace Catholics and that his father was non-verbal in expressing his emotions. The uneventful break was over and it was time for Richie to head back to college. His father drove him to the bus station and waited with him for the bus to arrive. As they sat on a bench waiting, a group of boys about Richie's age appeared and began to comment about Richie in stage whispers: "Repulsive!" "Fat Pig.... Disgusting...An insult to the human race...His parents must've cried when he was born..."

This went on until the bus arrived. Richie said good-bye, head down—not angry—just dejected. He never looked up to view his assailants. As his father assisted Richie with his bags, he suddenly turned to his son. He embraced him and kissed him and, in a voice strong and almost thunderous, said, "Richie, your mother and I are proud of you. I love you and could never have wanted more of a son than you." His father gave Richie another hug and kiss, and then left as his son boarded the bus.

Not too many months later, Father Manning met with the college chaplain who told of his first meeting with Richie after the Christmas break. "I had not seen Richie for some months and when he appeared in my office, I hardly knew him." Richie was transformed. He was no longer the boy in baggy pants with his fly half open. He had lost weight. He was clean shaven and well-groomed. The chaplain said Richie told him that he was working with a speech therapist and was making passing grades. Finally, he said that he had begun to date a coed on campus.

Father Manning went on to state that the simple affirming act of unconditional love demonstrated by the father at the bus terminal had the power to bring about a conversion in the son.

Whether from the smallest gesture of concern or from years of caring giving, what we do or say can make a difference. I've been blessed in countless ways by countless people. Beginning with my parents and family, words and actions expressed in love have been the stimulus for my growing and loving. I reflect upon three minutes total that were expressed by two of my professors at Gettysburg Seminary. The first came from Dr. Abdel Ross Went, my history professor. He asked me to stay a minute after class. When I did, he spoke but one sentence: "Oravec, you're capable of much better work." That was all. It was not said in chastisement. Instead I heard it as words of love. I went from being a "C" to an "A" student.

Another professor also asked me to remain after class. This time it was my Old Testament professor, Dr. Jacob Myers, who asked, "Oravec, are you all right?" Nothing more. In both cases I was overcome with the realization that I was recognized as a person. Fifty-seven years later, I still remember those three minutes.

It is for each of us to have the heart and mind of Jesus, the gift of the transforming power of love. It is the gift that comes in the renewing of our minds. St. Paul wrote to the Christians in Rome, "Do not be conformed to this world, but be transformed by the renewing of your minds, so that you may discern what is the will of God, what is good and acceptable and perfect."

There is nothing more exciting than to discover that the kingdom is within our true selves. We are able to give the self in love to others. We are ready for sacrificial and sacramental love. Life lived in faith sees life as an opportunity to be ourselves and to love without condition. The sacrificial self is able to work miracles and go the extra mile without personal aggrandizement. The sacramental self becomes God's lover with the power to pass it on. It is our calling and our reason for being.

Remember the story of the little boy carrying his younger brother who is almost as big as he is. His well-known response was, "He's not heavy, he's my brother." Love in life sees no task too big or too heavy.

Again, the way we think about ourselves and about others has a great impact on the way we live our lives. When we see ourselves as nobodies we seek to diminish or put down others because they are different. It is important that we think well of ourselves. We are God's beloved children. We need to think of others as children of the heavenly father as well. When we see ourselves as loved by God and others, we have strength for the journey of life. When we know ourselves to be loved and accepted, we are able to discover the God within us; we are able to give ourselves in love to all others. It is then that we become "somebody."

CHAPTER 17
DON'T MEET THEIR EYES

Some years ago I spent three weeks in China. We traveled a good deal across this incredible country. Everywhere our bus stopped we were greeted by the poor and needy. Some had disabilities and most had a pleading look in their eyes. With outstretched hands they sought to capture our attention and good will. Gary (his English name), our guide, desiring to be helpful, counselled us by saying, "Don't meet their eyes. Just look away or at the ground. Just keep walking."

Jesus said just the opposite: "See them and treat them as neighbors." In this chapter, the stories of Jesus boldly state that kingdom living demands seeing and helping those in need. We are to be "doers" of the word and not "hearers" only.

The parable for this chapter is one of the best known of the stories Jesus told. It has come to be called the "Parable of the Good Samaritan." It appears in the tenth chapter of the gospel of Luke.

And behold, a lawyer stood up to put him to the test, saying, "Teacher, what shall I do to inherit eternal life?" He said to him, "What is written in the law? How do you read?" And he answered, "You shall love the Lord your God with all your heart, and with all your soul, and with all your strength, and with all your mind; and your neighbor as yourself." And he said to him, "You have answered right; do this and you will live."

But he, desiring to justify himself, said to Jesus, "And who is my neighbor?" Jesus replied, "A man was going down from Jerusalem to Jericho, and fell into the hands of robbers, who stripped him, beat him, and went away, leaving him half dead. Now by chance a priest was going down that road; and when he saw him, he passed by on the other side. So likewise a Levite, when he came to the place and saw him, he passed on the other side. But a Samaritan while traveling, came near him; and when he saw him, he was moved with pity. He went to him and bandaged his wounds, having poured oil and wine on them. Then he put him on his own animal, brought him to an inn, and took care of him. The next day he took out two denarii, gave them to the innkeeper, and said, 'Take care of him; and when I come back, I will repay you whatever more you spend.' Which of these three, do you think, was a neighbor to the man who fell into the hands of the robbers?" He said, "The one who showed him mercy." Jesus said to him, "Go and do likewise."

Instructing the listeners to show mercy was not the unusual part of the parable of the Good Samaritan. The admonition to love God and others was declared loudly through many pages of the Torah. Indeed, the ritual of carrying a small box containing the words of the Shema was a perpetual reminder of the need to love God. The unusual thing about this story was that the hero was a Samaritan. The Samaritans were not considered "neighbors" and were not entitled to hospitality. The Samaritans, though many were Jews, worshipped differently and were often married to non-Jewish women. Thus they were considered "half-breeds." Most who heard such words from Jesus would have marveled, but the Pharisees fumed. This man Jesus was upsetting the normal protocol.

Jesus' listeners were familiar with the setting of the beating and robbery. The road between Jerusalem and Jericho ran through a dangerous and foreboding land. They also understood why the priest and Levite felt constrained to pass by the wounded man. They knew that if either of the two temple officials had approached the man, and if he were dead, they would be required to repeat the long and expensive process of ritual cleansing. What his listeners did not understand was the role of the Samaritan as the "good neighbor."

In the days of Jesus there were many questions that stirred discussion and debate. The question here was, "Who is my neighbor?" Jesus complicates the story by adding the Samaritan and the two temple officials to the story. In spite of all their prejudices and knowledge of temple protocol, those who listened to the story agreed that the "good neighbor" could only have been the one who showed mercy. That this was the Samaritan—a Gentile, an enemy, one who was not considered a "neighbor"—must have caused the crowd to breathe a deep "Wow!"

Jesus ends his story by directing those who followed him to "go and do likewise." The great commandment that Jesus taught was "Love one another," and he included "loving your enemy." Love was the keynote. It implied showing mercy. By making the Samaritan the hero, Jesus told his listeners that the Samaritan, too, was a neighbor.

Love is a verb. It requires the person who would love to show it in action or behavior. Scripture states that we are to be "doers of the word." I delight in the statement of St. Francis where he said, "Preach the Gospel, and use words only if necessary." George Washington Carver also grasped the heart of love in action when he said, "Your actions speak so loud I can't hear what you're saying."

Love becomes action when the Good Samaritan stops to help. He sees the man, a fellow human being, beaten and left for dead. He tends to his wounds, using wine and oil. He puts him on his own donkey, takes him to an inn and cares for him. He pays the bill and says, "If it costs more than what I've given you, I'll pay you the next time I'm here."

The Samaritan didn't know the man. He knew nothing of his background, his thinking, or whether or not he would express proper appreciation. There were no preexisting conditions of friend or enemy; race, creed or color; rich or poor; sexual orientation; political persuasion; educational, national, or religious background. He only saw a man in need and that was enough.

How often do we ask questions such as, "Who will pay for it?" or "Why do they deserve our help?" I believe Jesus would be unhappy with the questions we ask today. The Good Samaritan didn't ask. Jesus had him see need. His heart was moved by the suffering of a fellow human being and he simply did what was necessary.

The action of love and compassion begins with the ability to see need and then respond to it. "Meet their eyes; see them, all of them, as persons, as brothers and sisters."

There is a story about a farming community where one of the families fell on hard times. A prayer meeting was called to pray about the matter. While the congregation was in prayer, a teen-aged boy pulled up to the church with a wagon full of food. "Dad couldn't come to the meeting," he called out to the gathered fellowship, "but he sent his prayers. They're out in the wagon." Love in action...

It is for those who would be part of the kingdom of God to have open eyes and see need. They then will open their hands and seek to help. They will look into the others' eyes and see them as children of God.

Henri Matisse, the great painter, communicates the essence of seeing courageously. He wrote: "To see is itself a creative operation, requiring an effort. Everything that we see in our daily life is more or less distorted by acquired habits, and this is perhaps more evident in an age like ours, when cinema, posters and magazines present us with a flood of ready-made images which are to the eye what prejudices are to the mind. The effort needed to see things without distortion takes something very much like courage."

Seeing is central to kingdom living. Jesus again illustrates this in the story of the rich man and Lazarus, Luke 16:19-21.

There was a rich man who was dressed in purple and fine linen and who feasted sumptuously every day. And at his gate lay a poor man named Lazarus, covered with sores, who longed to satisfy his hunger with what fell from the rich man's table; even the dogs would come and lick his sores.

The rich man passed by Lazarus daily but yet he never really saw him. He, like the priest and the Levite, passed by. Jesus calls our attention to our blindness toward the poor and the wretched souls whom the world passes by daily.

As a teenager, my son David played the part of Jacob Marley in *The Christmas Carol.* He spoke the lines to Scrooge that are, in effect, the words of Jesus: "Business-- mankind was my business, the common welfare was my business, charity, mercy, forbearance, benevolence were, all, my business. The dealings of my trade were but a drop of water in the comprehensive ocean of my business."

I remember, when I was about five years old, being with my mother in downtown Johnstown, Pennsylvania. The great depression was at its worst. Dad was out of work and we, like most families, were poor. As we walked along Main Street, across from the city park, we came across a man sitting on the sidewalk. He had no legs. Mother stopped and dug into her pocketbook to find a nickel or dime to give to the man. He smiled and said thanks. I remember still my mother's kindness and the man's gratitude all those many years ago. Jesus said, "As you have done it to one of the least of these who are members of my family, you did it to me.

It is for all of us to have our eyes checked. We need to discover how well we see the need that exists everywhere.

I close this chapter with a brief story of a Rabbi and some of his students. He asked his students, "When do we know that the night is ended and the new day begun?"

The students responded with, "Is it when you can tell a sheep from a goat?"

The Rabbi said, "No."

"Is it when you can tell the difference between an olive and a fig tree?"

Again the Rabbi replied, "No." Finally, after several more possibilities, he said, "It is the moment when you can look at a face you've never seen before and recognize the stranger as a brother or sister. Until that moment, no matter how bright the day, it is still night."

CHAPTER 18

LOVE IS A HARSH AND DREADFUL THING

In Dostoyevsky's novel, *The Brothers Karamazov*, father Zosima, an old Russian Orthodox monk near the end of his life, is daily sought out by pilgrims. On one occasion he is confronted by a wealthy woman racked with doubt about the existence of God. She asks how she can find certainty in matters of faith.

"There's no proving it," Father Zosima tells her, "though you can be convinced of it."

"How," she asks.

"By the experience of active love. Strive to love your neighbor actively and tirelessly. As you advance in love you will grow surer of the reality of God and of the immortality of your soul. If you attain to perfect self-forgetfulness in the love of your neighbor, then you will believe without doubt, and no doubt can possibly enter your soul. This has been tried. This is certain."

The woman says that she loves humanity to such an extent that sometimes she imagines abandoning everything and becoming a sister of mercy, binding up wounds, even kissing them; but she wonders whether those she serves would be grateful or whether, instead, they might not respond with complaints and abuse. Dreading ingratitude, she does nothing.

Father Zosima tells her, "Love in action is a harsh and dreadful thing compared with love in dreams. Love in dreams thirsts for immediate action, rapidly performed and in the sight of all...but active love is labor and fortitude."

In the story of the Good Samaritan Jesus illustrated what a good neighbor would do: Show mercy. It demonstrated love in action. It was positive. All who heard Jesus' story answered with one voice that he who demonstrated mercy was the good neighbor.

Normally we think of love as being a positive force. This love cares about the well-being of those who are hurt or who have special needs.

In this chapter I explore another dimension of love. I call it "harsh love." Often this love appears to be a contradiction of the definition of love. This love is called upon for a different kind of need. It is indeed a love that is a "harsh and dreadful thing." Many shy away from this love because it is often confrontational and challenging. It may appear unloving and critical. It is, nevertheless, another dimension of the all-giving love we normally think of when we hear or see a need.

Here I take license to make some changes to the story Jesus told in the parable of the Good Samaritan. What if the Samaritan had arrived an hour or so earlier while the robbers were beating the poor traveler? How would Jesus have changed the response of the Good Samaritan?

- The Good Samaritan would have called 911.
- He would have waited until the robbers had gone and then come to help.
- He would have risked life and limb in an attempt to stop the robbers, possibly getting killed himself or killing one of the robbers.

He had to make a decision and time was of the essence.

Every day we make decisions and these decisions are a reflection of us and our values. Even no decision is a decision. Our lives are thus filled with the need to decide, to make a choice of action. When we confront behavior that we believe steals away from a God-given gift, our humanity, it calls for a loving but firm stand in opposition. It's a fine line between hating evil and yet still loving the embodiment of that evil.

In the story of the Good Samaritan Jesus is attacking the protocol of the day. The priest and the Levite were both officials in the temple. They decided to keep their distance from the beaten man because, as noted in the last chapter, if he were dead, they would have to repeat a very expensive cleansing process. Jesus' listeners were aware of this. Both men had the opportunity to stop and extend care to the victim but they decided that the rules of the temple were more important. Jesus is saying that they made a bad choice. Here again, Jesus is upsetting the temple rituals and rules—the accepted behavior of the day—in favor of showing mercy and of being a good neighbor.

This book is written with the perspective of Jesus being the ultimate benchmark in influencing our decisions. Consider the various motivations that usually affect our decisions and actions: the pain/pleasure principle which means selecting that which gives us the greatest pleasure and/or the least pain; the greatest good for the greatest number; tradition; or what people would think. All of these have great limitations. Jesus seeks to introduce a new way, the way of love. His way supersedes tradition, the greatest good for the greatest number, or personal gratification. His way establishes a new groundwork from which to decide.

Values based on love provide guidelines for action but don't dictate the particulars for our responses. I pose a scene that is extreme, yet helpful, in identifying the difficulty of decision-making.

Suppose you hear a loud knocking at your front door late at night. You answer the door and discover a rough, out-of-control group of armed men. To say they were up to no good is to understate the situation. Your wife and children are upstairs sleeping peacefully. In a split second it becomes apparent that your entire household is in jeopardy. The men push you aside as they move into the house and head upstairs. There is no time to call for help. You can tell that the men are beyond rational dialogue and would not listen to your pleas. You have a hunting gun in the closet. You must make a quick decision whether to get it and defend your family, possibly killing one of the men or being killed yourself, or to do nothing. What do you do?

Detrick Bonhoeffer was a Lutheran pastor during the time of Adolf Hitler's rise to power. All his life Bonhoeffer had been a pacifist, but he was strongly opposed to Hitler's persecution of the Jews. He saw the evil that was being done and joined a group that was plotting to assassinate Hitler. Because of his concern for the safety of his family, Bonhoeffer counselled the group but did not take part in the actual attempt. Nevertheless he was eventually hung for his part in the unsuccessful plot.

Could it be that Jesus, the Prince of Peace, would suggest that the Good Samaritan use brute force or maybe even kill in the defense of the man being beaten? It is an awful thought to remember that the Christians of Germany did not stand in unity to protest what was happening to the Jewish population. Thankfully, many individuals did protest and help; but as a country, they did not.

There is no general rule about love and what it can or cannot do. The situation determines what active love would direct. At times it is, indeed, harsh love.

Harsh love can't help but be part of the expression of love. Unconditional love is not a license to do whatever we please, but it is a framework for every relationship. Again, there can be no fixed answer. Both my children were good children, but on a few occasions I had to decide whether to hug and talk, or give a strong no, perhaps with an added punishment. To hug or to reprimand is a dynamic of unconditional love and harsh love. The two expressions are of one overriding love.

Few question that we are to be lovers of peace, and yet scriptures tell us that God "hates evil." It seems to me that we must be ready to do what's necessary to stop evil, to stop what is hurtful to "the least of these, my brothers." At times, in a broken world with evil abounding, we may kill in love; but this must be the court of last resort. If it becomes a way of life, we have lost our way. Walter Winkle, in his book, *Engaging the Powers*, poses the question, "How can we oppose evil without creating new evils and being made evil ourselves?"

It is a risk we must take, as we seek to be faithful to the Spirit of God as our guide.

We will not be called on to join a plot to assassinate an evil leader. We will have, however, countless opportunities to act against the vast array of intolerance, bigotry, prejudice, and all manner of evil in the world. Over the years I've said to myself, "I'm intolerant of intolerance."

All of us are given the opportunity, at one time or another, to oppose evil; and it usually comes in concrete situations. We need to be ready to say the defending word or commit some action.

That reminds me of an anecdote I can't help but include here: There is a story about a seminary professor who understood "harsh love." He was known for his commitment to unconditional love. He taught it, he preached it and he wrote about it. One day he was out in front of his house mending a broken sidewalk. He was just sweeping up when some of his students stopped by for a chat. As they stood admiring their professor's good work, a group of teen-aged boys came racing around the corner and managed to run straight through the newly-laid concrete. In a flash the professor was after them, broom in hand. When he returned, the students were waiting with impish grins on their faces. They asked the professor, "What happened to unconditional love?"

He responded with an equally impish grin, "In the abstract, yes; in the concrete, no."

Harsh love: It is not defensive but proactive and creative. It wants the best for the object of that love. It is not a manipulative love seeking its own ends. It is most certainly not an angry or resentful love. Yet it has teeth in it that often appear unloving, especially to the object of that action. It is compassionate, yet it spells out what may appear to be harsh demands and the rationale for them.

Harsh love means always to confront and oppose that which is not in the spirit of unconditional love. Christians in particular must act according to the heart and mind of Jesus and not by orthodoxy. I began this chapter wondering what Jesus would have said if the Good Samaritan had arrived on the scene an hour or two earlier when the traveler was being beaten. I believe that our broken world will, unfortunately, present us with such hard decisions in life. Our dilemma is that we must seek to act in the most loving way, the way that may reap the best results. Yet the issues are deep and complex and thus extremely difficult.

Earlier I said that war or war-like behavior in daily life should be the court of last resort, and no wonder. Look at the dramatic statistics cited in a Washington Post article (4/27/2014). By the close of World War 1 in 1918, 15,000,000 people had been killed. By 1945, the death toll from two world wars had passed 100,000,000. After the nuclear arms race had begun, a U.S. war games model suggested in 1983 that an all-out battle with the Soviet Union would kill a billion people in the first few weeks. At that time, that meant one human in five would perish.

There are the "Hawks" and there are the "Doves." There is little question that Jesus would be a Dove. "Blessed are the peacemakers for they shall be called the children of God."

As I've said before, love is a verb; it is an action. It is proactive. It seeks out and responds to need, whether a person's need, a community's or a nation's. It is for us to move in the direction of being a good neighbor.

Leo Tolstoy, as a child, was told by his older brother that there was a green stick buried in the forest some-where in Russia. The stick had printed on it the words that would bring peace and harmony to the world. Tolstoy never found the stick but he never forgot it. Near the end of his life he still believed in such a stick with the words of salvation for humankind.

St. John of the Cross uttered some possible words for the green stick. He said, "Love is the measure by which we shall be judged.

As we walk the way of the Lord, there are times when the absolute becomes clouded by what we see and hear. We are to love our enemy and all that that implies; yet there will be times when we need to confront another. The values put forth in the teachings of Jesus must un-dergird the motives of the Christian or God-centered person. War should never be the first choice. But when time is of the essence, we need to act.

If we have eyes to see, we recognize evil in our world. It is often not enough to only speak out against it. It is a call to become active in love, a call for "labor and fortitude." In general our posture needs to be that of seeking peace, yet there are always situations that call for more than words and good will.

I end this chapter by stating there is no easy answer. We are called upon to be involved, to be creatively part of the answer and not of the problem.

CHAPTER 19

A WORD FROM THE LIGHTHOUSE

Steven Covey, in one of his books, tells a story about a great ship of the sea. As I recall, it went something like this: One afternoon a communication was received reading "Change course." The message was taken to the proud captain who scoffed and responded, "You change course." Shortly another message with greater emphasis arrived: "Change course now!" Upon receiving that message, the captain was really miffed. He responded, "This is the greatest ship of the seas. You change course!" Very shortly a third message arrived which read, "This is the lighthouse. Change course."

It's a delightful story about pride and presumption. It illustrates the old adage, "Pride goeth before a fall."

The captain's know-it-all attitude had the potential for disaster. The human race seems to have a built-in state of presumption and pride that assumes an ability to know what's best. The Frank Sinatra song "I Did It My Way" expresses some inner need for individuality and the merit of not following the herd. The danger is that pride and self-centeredness can be the stuff of our individual loss in the living of our days. When we, as individuals, assume we know best, we challenge the eternal.

The final parable that I include in this little book is a good summary when considering the wisdom that Jesus shared in his stories. It appears in the seventh chapter of Matthew, verses 24-27.

Everyone that hears these words of mine and acts on them will be like a wise man who built his house on rock. The rain fell, floods came, the winds blew and beat on that house, but it did not fall, because it was founded on rock. And everyone who hears these words of mine and does not act on them will be like a foolish man who built his house on sand. The rains fell and the floods came and the winds blew and beat against that house, and it fell, and great was its fall.

The captain, like the man who built his house on sand, was foolish. Neither felt any need for further guidance beyond what their own limited perception provided. The man with a solid foundation knows that he can

weather the storms of life. In his parable, Jesus is telling
us that faith and trust in God and God's unconditional
love form the foundation on which we should build our
lives.

Jesus came as a rabbi, a teacher; and the stories he
told were not for entertainment. They were meant to be
heard and then put into practice. The kingdom of God
is not a spectator sport. We are not to watch from the
sidelines but are invited to play in the game. So build a
house we must, or sometimes change course if we must,
but do it with a firm foundation of faith and trust in
God's unconditional love. In the end, it is a trust relationship we are invited to participate in, a relationship
illustrated by this story:

A little girl was trapped on the second floor of a
burning building. Her father was down below. He told
her to jump from the window and that he would catch
her. She recognized her father's voice and knew she
could trust him and his love for her. Confidence in her
father's ability to catch her was the critical ingredient in
the child's leap of courage.

Another story I often told my students about the
faith and trust factor had to do with a high-wire aerialist. He was preparing to take a high-wire walk across
the Niagara Falls. A large crowd had come to greet him.
Among the gathering was a teen-aged boy. As the boy
was getting his autograph, the aerialist asked him if he
believed he could walk the tightrope across the falls.

The youngster enthusiastically replied, "Yes, I believe I could."

Then the aerialist asked, "Do you trust me enough to get in this little wheelbarrow here and let me push you across?" The boy's faith became shaky!

It is critical to know the voice of one who bids us to jump or to climb into the wheelbarrow. Trusting takes courage—a leap of faith. Jesus said, *"I am the way, the truth, and the life..."* In him and in his life we discover our true selves.

Here is a story by Soren Kierkegaard that calls us to live life fully.

"There was a flock of geese imprisoned in a barnyard surrounded by a tall fence. One day, a preaching goose came into their midst. He stood on an old crate and admonished the geese for being content with this confined, earthbound existence. He recounted the exploits of their forefathers who spread their wings and flew the trackless wastes of the sky. He spoke of the goodness of the Creator who had given the geese the urge to migrate and the wings to fly. This pleased the geese. They nodded their heads and marveled at these things and applauded the eloquence of the preaching goose. All this they did, but the one thing they never did, they did not fly. They went back to their waiting dinner, for the corn was good and the barnyard secure."

It takes courage to fly. Risk is part of the faith factor. We need to have faith that if we open our wings we will fly. Only then will we experience our true calling. As we walk in the way of kingdom living, we gain strength and confidence. Jesus, in a sense, challenges his hearers to "Come fly with me." The joy of life is made full as we learn to fly and claim our destiny.

Jesus bids us to select wisely the foundations upon which our lives are based. He not only teaches the way, he is the way that leads to the whole or abundant life. He is the lighthouse. He is the rock.

CHAPTER 20
THE JOURNALS OF THE PRODIGAL COME HOME

The journals of the prodigal began the day after the party to celebrate his homecoming. They reflect some of the issues that kingdom living represents.

Martin Luther said that the Christian life is a process of becoming. Thus, as we observe the struggle to "become" in the prodigal, we also observe the struggles of every person.

We are in the kingdom. The prodigal was home and yet he was not yet "what he shall be." We are the children of the heavenly father through his unconditional love, and yet maturity is a life-long process. "Be you perfect as your heavenly father is perfect," is a process of becoming.

The journals here are but a snippet of life, illustrating the messages put forward in this book. Each of us can identify our personal issues of becoming.

My Journal

I'm wide awake. Exhausted, but so wired that sleep is impossible. Dad told me to sleep in tomorrow, all day. I may end up doing just that.

It feels so good to be home. I'm happy to be here, but I can't get my head around what happened.

I knew Dad was a good guy, but never, in my wildest dreams did I think he would do what he did. Running out to meet me, crying and laughing, and saying over and over, "My son, my son." I was stunned, didn't know what to do. He didn't even give me time to say I'm sorry.

I feel some sleep coming on. Thank you...

The sleep was sweet. I haven't slept that well in years. Finally got up in time for lunch. Mom and Dad had already eaten so they just sat with me, both of them not saying a lot, kind of just looking at me and smiling. I was starving and ate more than I had in months.

Thinking about the party... It was a big deal. Everyone seemed to be there. It was upbeat. Dad was the life of the party; he even sang and danced with the music.

I just couldn't get over how happy everyone was to see me. I expected the opposite. I deserved the opposite.

One downer came after Dad went out in the yard for a while. I didn't know it, but my brother got home from work and he wouldn't come in. Some things never change. It seemed to upset Dad, but he got back into the celebration.

A whole day back home. Never believed I would ever be this happy to be home.

I'm feeling rested up. Been sleeping a lot. My ol' bod is in bad shape. I shudder when I think back. The fact that I'm alive is some kind of miracle.

Trying to process Dad. Either he's different or I'm different, but—how do I put this—he really likes me— or better still—he really seems to love me. Can't figure it out, after the way I acted. Don't understand.

Bed time. Thanks.

I've been home a week now and I feel the need to do something. I've been trying to get Dad to tell me what he wants me to do. He's not all that helpful. He just says, "You're part of the family, my son. Just be my son."

I don't quite know what that means.

━◁┼┼▷━

Dad keeps saying there is something more than rules. When I ask him, he says, "The rules are like curbs. They keep us on the road, or give us a bump when we run over one; but whether we stay on the road or go astray, something is always with us." But then he doesn't tell me what that something is.

━◁┼┼▷━

Watching Dad gives me a good idea about my question on rules. It's more of being a certain way. I'm watching him closely and listening to what he says to me and to other people and the way he says it.

━◁┼┼▷━

I've had some frustrating days. Seems like I should be doing better. Talked to Dad about it. He smiled and asked if I remembered all the times I'd asked, "Are we there yet?" when we were on a trip. He asked if I remembered the answer he gave. I said I did: "We're not there yet, but we're on the way." I got the point.

━◁┼┼▷━

Some tough thoughts...I was away, far away...might even say out of this world away. Makes me feel bad. Wasted—I just wasted three years. I guess the good thing is that I learned to appreciate...the hard way. I wouldn't suggest that way of learning appreciation.

≈⟨⟩≈

Another week has gone by and I've just been hanging out. Helping Mom a little around the house. She's been catching me up on some of the things that happened during the three years I was gone.

Every now and then I hear something from one of the servants that upsets me, about how tough it was for Mom and Dad while I was away. Makes me feel big-time bad...

Tomorrow Dad and I are getting together for a meeting. I asked if it would be okay for us to meet and talk. He smiled and said, "Great. How about 9:00." I have a lot of stuff that I just can't figure out. Maybe Dad can help.

Time for sleep. Thanks

≈⟨⟩≈

After breakfast Dad and I went for a long walk and then sat out in the vineyard. I had all kinds of questions to ask about what I was feeling and—well—a lot of stuff.

Dad kind of broke the ice and talked about what a great party it was and how delighted everyone was to see me. He said that everyone came up and congratulated him and his good fortune. His good fortune... that blows my mind. I'm the one with the good fortune.

In the middle of our talking I just all of a sudden started to cry. I used to hide my tears when I was younger; it was like I wanted to hide myself. Now I was sobbing and wiping my eyes. Dad handed me a handkerchief. I blew my nose and said, "I'm so happy to be home. Thank you."

He gave me a hug and said, "You have brought gladness back into our hearts." He asked if I wanted to go out into the fields with him tomorrow.

Thanks. Sleep time. Thanks

Dad and I spent the day together. I can't write how good I felt. I was more relaxed than I can remember. Every now and then we stopped and did some work. He never had to say, "Come and help me." I just felt I should—it was such a natural thing to do. I thought back to before I left home. Then I hated anything out in the fields.

I'm trying to figure out what's happened to me— why I've changed. I know that being away turned out to be a hard trip, but it's more than just the downer of the last three years.

Looking forward to tomorrow. Thanks. Sleep.

※ ※

I'm really not sure what's happening to me. It's like I'm losing it or something. I walk around all day being happy, smiling most of the time.

When I was away, there were a lot of good times. We carried on, lots of beer and stuff; but this is something deeper—kind of coming from down deep somewhere—just being home and hanging out with Dad. I'm having another of my meetings with Dad tomorrow.

Sleep. Thanks.

※ ※

Meeting with Dad today. I talked a lot, shared some of my feelings. I told him about being glad and sad at the same time. I'm glad to be home, but, wow, when I think about the last three years, all the bad stuff and wasting all the money—well, I told him how guilty I feel, how unworthy. I told him that I didn't understand his attitude towards me. I told him I felt the need to make up for all the pain and everything that I caused.

After a long pause I said, "I don't feel right wearing the ring. It's not right that I'm in the house. I should be out with the hired help. I need to do something to make up—to earn—

I talked a lot. It all just kind of rolled out of me. Dad listened. I felt it was okay to let it all hang out. The way he looked at me made me feel okay.

Hard day. Sleep. Thanks.

Was out with Dad all day. We worked. He's most often on the quiet side. He just hands me a bucket and I know what he wants. So I fill it up with water and take it to some of the smaller stock. Or he opens the barn door, and the next thing I know we're carrying hay together or fixing a hinge or repairing a rig. It's so natural doing things with Dad.

I like to watch him and listen to him when he's with the other workers. Secretly I'm studying how he does it so that I might learn and sometime do the same.

Tired. A very good tired. Sleep. Thanks.

Tonight as I began to write in my journal I noticed that I was ending my journal entries with "Thanks." I thought a long time about what that meant. It seemed like a natural thing to do--almost like something I had to do. Thanks. I remembered back to the day when the big insight came—the day I was so low that it didn't matter if I lived or died. Then something deep inside me said, "Help."

I'd forgotten about that in the excitement of coming home. I'm starting to understand some of it.

As I reflect on what all has happened since that time, I now write "Thanks" in a very different way, with a better idea of who I'm thanking.

━✦✦━

My brother and I just didn't get along. He was always telling me how much better he was in everything. He is older by three and a half years, so he was always able to beat me up. Well, anyway, he made me feel lousy about myself and most of the time I was mad at him. I guess since I've been home I've been hoping that he'd come and apologize to me. But he is still as bad as I remember. I'm going to keep hoping.

━✦✦━

Dad and I talked about my brother. This is one of the hard things for me. He's still—well, I'll try to be good and not write what I'm thinking. Let's just say he lives in his world and his world is always right. Over the years he seemed to get pleasure from putting me down—as if putting me down builds him up somehow.

I'm trying to understand my feelings and what part I've played in where the two of us are. I've been doing a lot of work on me, thinking and trying to understand.

It's great to be around Dad. I can say just about anything and, even when he disagrees with where I am on something, I don't feel judged by him. Yet I know I'm not where I need to be.

Long day. Sleep. Thanks.

———※┼ ┼※———

How could I have been so wrong and yet felt that I was absolutely right? When I think back to the time I was getting ready to leave home, I don't think anyone could have convinced me that I was wrong. Early on, both Mom and Dad had talked with me about my general attitude but I just tuned them out. I'm not sure what happened but now it's hard for me to see myself the way I was. I just couldn't see it their way. I think Dad realized that and in the last months he felt he had to let me go and learn the hard way. I did.

Sleep. Thanks.

———※┼ ┼※———

I shared with Dad for the first time my experience in the pig pen, when I was so low I thought about killing myself. I asked someone—anyone—to help me. . I shared how I cried myself to sleep. When I woke up everything was different. I knew I was going to be all right. I don't know how I knew, but I knew. That very day I headed for home. Now I know that the "someone" was God.

≈⧸⊹⧹≈

As time has passed, I've felt a power coming out of the inner part of me...as if I were a new me, a true me...

≈⧸⊹⧹≈

I'll never forget, or at least, I don't think I will ever forget my three years away; but the memory has no power over me. There is nothing that draws me in that direction—no "I wish I were still there" thoughts. Something deep in me has worked a miracle. I'm sure it started when I asked for help in the pig pen...God in me...I think so...

≈⧸⊹⧹≈

At first, after I got home and had the party and all, I thought everything would change, and it did; but it was just the beginning and not the end. I felt new, but there was still my brother, and there was still all the stuff in me that had to be dug out.

≈⧸⊹⧹≈

Strange, how God came when my world was as dark as could be...in the pig pen...at the bottom. Maybe my defenses had to go so he could come. I'm just thankful, even for the pig pen.

"Darkest before dawn," somebody said.

———

When I was growing up I learned the Torah. I learned, too, about Hosea and the love of God; but I thought it was a lot of stuff. Seemed like if you believed all that stuff, it would spoil your fun. How wrong, how wrong.

———

I would die for my Dad. Yes I would. He above all I not only love, but I trust and have faith in him.

———

Payoff time—the fun part—giving myself away, helping Mom and Dad and wherever I'm needed. I feel almost giddy inside as I think of how good it is, doing good things because I am who I am, my father's son. I am a child of God.

———

When I was in the pig pen people didn't see me. They were there, but I was a nobody. They treated me like dirt. People put me in a slot. I was a born slob in the pig pen, dirty, poor, and a kind of "it." I remember, boy do I remember, what it felt like being an "it."

I already felt like dirt and they only confirmed what I felt. I felt like a thing and it was a bad feeling. I vowed that if I had another chance I would look at people and be aware of people, all kinds of people.

Dad talked about enemies today. If I'm honest, my brother has been my enemy. He's never been kind to me. When I was little he hurt me physically and has always abused me. He made fun of me and put me down around the family and neighbors. I think I've always hated him.

Dad is working on my head and my heart. Reflecting on how it was when I came home, I'm starting to get the point. I was a nobody and Dad treated me like a somebody, his son. I think he's trying to tell me that now I need to treat my brother...wow...like Dad treated me.

Dad helps me go deep inside myself. Every time we get together, some way or other he's nudging me to look inside before I look outside for answers. It's so easy to blame others—my brother, other people, really, the world.

During my pigpen days I lost confidence and gave up hope of any kindness from people. Easy to do. But Dad says it's a judgmental attitude so I'm working on it. He loves to say, "Better to light one candle than curse the darkness."

The more I see me, deep inside, the closer to God I feel. It's a lot of me coming together, feeling better. It's like I'm getting to be, how do I put it, the real me. I like my feelings. It makes me not as mad at my big brother.

———

I really, really want to please Dad. He tells me, though, that what will really please him is when I'm able to naturally do good and think good, without trying to please him.

———

I had a bad dream last night. My brother was choking me and laughing. Dad said I might just be my brother in the dream. That's scary.

———

Dad said today, "Doing bad things does not make us bad persons." I believe that a lot of people think just the opposite. When people saw me I could read their thoughts: "Here comes that boy who caused his parents all that grief. He was in the far country for three years..." Except they don't mean "far country." They think "sin city." And they're right. Or are they? Or is Dad right?

━◁╂▷━

I wonder what life would be like if I had never gone off to the far country and stayed home instead. Would I have ended up like my brother? I sure hope not.

The "what ifs" of life. I'll never know. I certainly can't recommend the far country to anyone. For me, I was blessed that somehow I came to myself before it was too late. A lot of people never come back from the far country.

I guess, if I had a wish, I would wish I could have gotten to know my dad earlier. It's too bad that I had so much baggage—my brother—my old friends—my hormones— influencing me the wrong way.

If I'd had anything like my current relationship with Dad, I'm positive my life would have taken a different turn, a different road...

━◁╂▷━

Part of that time was the rock and the hard place. To leave home ended up as a bad decision. But if I had stayed and nothing had changed in me, it would have been more of the same. My brother and I just might have killed each other. Well, at least it would have been a hard time.

We do the best we know how at any given time, even when things are really bad. How do we improve "the best I could do?" How do we grow up to make better decisions?

The "could have, should have" is easy after the fact. Looking back now, I know what I should have done; but that was not in my plans then.

I'm convinced that I have to improve, to be better and work harder. It seems to me that I have to prove myself. I feel a great sense of urgency, almost like a drive.

Dad keeps telling me that I didn't have to pay my way. He once said to me, "I'm not for sale. I love you because you are my son, not because you are good."

Dad loves to kid me by saying, "I love you for nothing, and now you can be good for nothing." Today in our session together I was telling Dad about some of my work, the fun I was having, and that nobody told me I had to do it. He laughed and said, "It's nice when you can be good for nothing." I have to think about that, being good for nothing-- although I'm starting to get the idea.

＝≍+ +≍＝

My brother and I seem to be getting along better. I'm not sure why but I'll take it any way I can get it.

＝≍+ +≍＝

I met a girl in town and I'm psyched! Nice-looking. We'll see...

＝≍+ +≍＝

I've been thinking about my sex drive. After the far country, I've come to see that it is more special than I than I had given it credit for. I really treated it too casually, just for thrills; but it meant nothing to me.

＝≍+ +≍＝

Today I had a major breakthrough. I suddenly realized that all these years it was not all my brother's fault. I had more to do with it than I thought. I remembered a lot of things, attitude-type things, things I did that put me in the right and him in the wrong. I'm kind of astonished. I wonder how often I've done that.

━━†⊹†━━

Still seeing my girlfriend in town…

━━†⊹†━━

I feel a lot of guilt about my past and am still wanting to make up for the damage I caused, the people I hurt.

Dad listened to all of this. He finally said, "It's hard when you hurt people you love. Your mother and I were not so much hurt as we were concerned and worried about you. We loved you so much that we could not help caring about you. Yes, it was a hard time for us; but our pain was not anger at you but love for you."

"It was a love pain that we experienced. You are now experiencing love pain of a different kind. It's a love pain because of the hurt you caused those you love."

I interrupted Dad and asked, "But how do I get rid of feeling so bad? "

He replied, "To have remorse is painful. There is no avoiding it and it should not be avoided. Yet, while the past cannot be undone, the present and future are helped because you have been changed by the past."

"So I have to live with the remorse?" I asked.

"Yes and no. Yes, there is no avoiding the past and, as I said, there should be no desire to avoid it. We love and accept you as you are. You must move on, allowing your past experiences to help guide you in the future."

<hr />

"This is the first day of the rest of your life" is a phrase I'd heard many times, but now it has a special meaning for me. I can't get rid of my past life but I'm able to begin a new life because of Dad's love for me. He has made it possible for me to live again. If he hadn't loved and forgiven me, I'd be trapped."

Dad called it "love pain." It's hard for me to realize how I failed and hurt Mom and Dad and others. It's strange that when I was in the grips of leaving that I didn't think of anyone. Only my needs were important.

<hr />

Major insight came to me today, one I will always remember. I realized that Dad's love for me has made it possible for me to be a loving person. The more I receive his love, the more I love myself and the more love I have to give.

That is a super big WOW.

<hr />

I've discovered that on the days when I begin to concentrate on what I was like in the far country and how unworthy I feel to be home now, it seems to draw power out of me, like a thief. I know where I've been but I'm not there anymore. I need to keep my eye on the future, not on the past.

Dad has encouraged me to reflect on some of the lessons I learned as a boy—things I memorized from the Torah and the teachings of the rabbi.

Our neighbor Sam is an older guy and super nice man. He was upset today because his best working horse fell into a sink hole and they weren't able to get him out. Before Sam could finish what he was saying, Dad was walking toward the barn. In what seemed like the blink of an eye, he had three of our horses hitched to the wagon and we were heading down the road. In a very short time, we pulled the horse to safety and I learned a lesson about being a good neighbor. When Sam attempted to pay my dad, he refused, saying, "My pleasure, neighbor." It felt good.

Dad keeps saying, "Look within." He has said that so often during our talks. Most of my life I've been looking out there, at other people, the good life, success...

But Dad has kept after me and I'm beginning to understand. What is real for me? It seems that God has given me a capacity to know, if only I will take the time and make the effort to find it...

〰️

Today Dad said, "I know you want me to tell you how to act and how to think. But this is a time for you to discover things inside you and not outside. We'll talk about the outside stuff soon enough, but right now keep working on the inside."

The "inside" stuff...what does Dad mean? I thought and thought and then it came to me that those were the things I experienced within: coming to myself, coming home, and the answer I got while I was in the pigpen— the answer to my plea for help...

There was a connection...

〰️

Today I've been thinking about my lack of insight into myself. How come I had and continue to have less than perfect vision? I'm much better than I was, but now I can only hope that my insight will continue to improve. As people get older, their eyesight becomes less than perfect but in the spiritual realm, it should improve.

How could I have seen bad as good and be so convinced I was right?

I've decided that part of the reason I left home was ignorance—ignorance being a state of not knowing. The interesting question for me is, why couldn't I hear Mom and Dad? Maybe the best I can do is to say, "I don't know but I know that I couldn't or wouldn't hear them.

The thief who steals knows the law and knows that stealing is wrong, but is convinced that it will lead to the good life.

I've never wanted to kill my brother, but I remember reading about Cain and Abel—a brother killing his brother. I understand anger and maybe hate. Where do they come from and why? Sin? I was angry because I thought my brother had messed up my world—my little, self-centered world...

It's interesting how different my attitude has become. I just see things differently now. I look at people in a different way, as though I never saw them before. My brother is a perfect example. Until I started to really listen to him, hear him, and get in touch with his views, I never "saw" him.

I've begun to feel free to hear and see almost everyone differently. It's wonderful.

I've been trying to listen to my big brother, trying to let go of my anger and trying not to defend myself when he throws a barb. Dad said, "Good. Keep it up," when I told him what I was trying to do.

Something really strange happened to me today. I've been working hard on listening to my brother. I've been working on it for a few months now, keeping a lid on me and my emotions—just listening and saying "Ahh," or "really?" Now a really, really weird thing is happening. We're starting to get along. I'd never bet a nickel on its happening, but I'm starting to like him. Even more incredible, I think he's starting to like me!

I told Dad about what I realized about my brother and me yesterday. He broke out in one of the biggest smiles I've ever seen on him. He gave me the thumbs-up sign. It warmed me all over to see that smile.

━◁┼ ┼▷━

Today was a day that almost puts me at a loss for words. My brother and I have been making progress in our relationship but I never expected that he would ask for a time when we could talk. That was unusual. We could talk anytime. When we got together, he shared how much it's meant to him for us to be brothers, and even friends. He told me how much he resented me when I came back and was treated like a hero. Then he said something that brought tears to my eyes. He said, "I need for you to forgive me."

Through my tears I said I did and then, also what I didn't expect, I asked him to forgive me. I'd been angry with him for a long time...

━◁┼ ┼▷━

Little by little I've been finding me...and feeling I'm okay. Just to be me is fine. I'm not my brother. I'm not any of my friends. I'm part of Dad, but even there, I'm still just ol' me. I'm starting to handle that. Strange how

I've avoided what's right in my face...wanting to be like someone else. Guess I wasn't satisfied with me.

Dad said again, "Keep looking in." More and more I'm getting the message.

＝‡ ‡＝

Dad's acceptance of me when I came home helped me make the trip inside myself. He accepted me and loved me even when I was a total mess.

＝‡ ‡＝

Needing to prove something to myself or to others... that was my thinking today. Prove to everyone that I could. Could what? I don't even know what that means. Leave home, get my inheritance early, waste it... It still hurts to think that Dad gave it to me and I blew it.

＝‡ ‡＝

Dad says that we are like a ball of energy, and the energy was meant for us to live the life that God meant for us. Anger, envy, defensiveness, lying and trying to impress others all steal away our energy. Because of these thieves, we have less energy for living. I only know that pretending to be something I'm not wastes a lot of energy, maybe even seventy-five percent. That would leave only twenty-five percent to use on being the true me.

＝⟨+ +⟩＝

The more I'm at peace with myself, the more I seem to get along with other people. I have to admit they seem to like me better.

Before I left home I felt Dad was not really in touch. He was old and couldn't possibly understand. I laugh now at how differently I see him. Strange how that happens.

＝⟨+ +⟩＝

My brother and I are getting along better than ever. We laugh together, saying "Who do we blame our problems on now?" I still do it, blaming something outside myself for my problems; but I'm catching myself more.

＝⟨+ +⟩＝

There's something really healthy about taking responsibility for my life and not blaming home, or my brother, or, or...

＝⟨+ +⟩＝

Just got back from some time with Dad. He said it was time to move on from the blame game—blaming myself and others. He said, "When you are forgiven, your job or task is to accept the forgiveness." That's still a hard thing for me to do.

✂┼┼✂

Dad said something that I've not thought about before. He said, "There is a whole history to consider: yours and the family's." I've been so caught up in trying to figure out what's right for me that I haven't thought of much beyond that, like our family and what we believe in. I've been remembering a lot of things about when I was growing up. I need to pay more attention to all that.

✂┼┼✂

A subject that keeps pushing on me is the question of my God. I was brought up to believe and to trust, but somewhere along the way I lost it. Two things, though—my experience in the pig pen and the "thank you" endings in my earlier journals—have brought the question front and center.

✂┼┼✂

Had an interesting talk with Dad this morning. I was able to tell him how much I love and respect him, and that my goal in life is to be just like him.

He paused for a long time and then gave me something to think about. He said, "I appreciate your love for me and that you want to be like me. You are my son and indeed there are marks that I have given you that I hope are part of who you are."

He paused again and then continued, "But the most important thing for you is to be you—my son, yes, but the special, unique you."

He also talked about a way of being rather than the way of strict obedience. He said that just obeying the laws blindly can be dangerous. A way of "being" is more important. He mixes up my head!

I must've known deep inside me that the values, the things that really count were not in that far country. I'm beginning to accept all of me. As I think of my past compared with my thoughts and feelings now, I realize that I'm not just good or bad. I'm both. But I know I'm moving in the right direction. Little by little, I'm feeling like my inside and outside are finally getting together.

Strangely, when I see myself clearly I feel like I'm getting closer to God. I know I'm thankful he brought me home...

EPILOGUE

The controlling principle of the cosmos I believe to be unquestionably the power of unconditional love. In a sick and broken world where evil is visible on all sides, the power of love does battle. I believe the embodiment of this eternal power was manifest in the person of Jesus. Is it the green stick sought by Tolstoy? Is it the magic bullet, the cure-all sought by multitudes throughout history? I believe so.

If we discovered a cure for the common cold and had a pill that would bring relief, it would do no good if the person didn't take it. How do we convince the world that accepting and giving unconditional love is the answer?

Two thousand years is evidence that this is not going to happen easily. In the time that we and future generations will live, it is for each of us to personally become the embodiment of this eternal truth. It will change the world. Each person who embraces this controlling principle—this living word as it is witnessed in the Christ of God—holds the power to transform his or her small part of the universe. The repercussions and waves are as the flapping of a butterfly's wings in China sending a storm across the sea.

Will it bring the change needed? It is not for us to know. It is only for us to flap our wings.

SOME AFTERTHOUGHTS

My purpose in writing these chapters is not unlike Paul's, as he wrote in Colossians 2:2-3:

> *"My goal is that they may be encouraged in heart and united in love, so that they may have the full riches of complete understanding, in order that they may know the mystery of God, namely, Christ, in whom are hidden all the treasures of wisdom and knowledge."*

Seeing Jesus through his stories sheds more light on his values than all the creeds proclaimed by the church and stories of his life as described in the scriptures.

Implications of Unconditional Love

- Courage to be yourself. As we learn to love our-selves, warts and all, we become God's sacramen-tal selves, empowered to bring unconditional love to others. We become God's lovers.
- In marriage, when two people commit them-selves to each other, they are empowered to love through any difficulty.
- If congregations loved unconditionally, the con-flicts within the church could be reconciled with the commitment of the unconditional love of God in Christ.
- If we loved others unconditionally, seeking the good for others as well as ourselves, then even world situations could be worked through to resolution.
- If we refuse to accept God's unconditional love, we remove ourselves from the ultimate truth of the universe. In our separation we remain alone.
- Unconditional love—the gift of God and embod-ied in Jesus—is the power to rekindle our true humanity.

Jesus has given us a plan of action in the context of his love and life. But to paraphrase G. K. Chesterton,

Christianity has not been tried and found wanting, it has never been tried.

※⁘⁘※

Rabbi Jesus came with the promise for a new life and a new song. He gives us a song to sing in our daily lives, both in the good days and in days of hardship and sorrow. I love this old Chinese proverb:

"A bird does not sing because it has an answer. It sings because it has a song."

AFTERWORD
By David Oravec

Six months after Dad died I received a text that read "Hey Uncle David, it's your favorite nephew Matthew! I've been thinking about getting a small tattoo to remember Grandpa. Did he have a favorite scripture verse? One that he really loved?"

Clearly, as this wonderful little book shows, Dad had a favorite story from scripture: the parable of the Prodigal Son. That part was easy. But honing in on one verse required thought and some conjecture because Dad never articulated a specific line as a favorite. So, I wrote back to Matthew and told him I'd think it over.

This meant revisiting the parable and remembering the glow and joy on Dad's face when he talked about it. This meant re-reading the story that Dad believed Jesus loved to tell the most. The story is only captured by Luke, the physician, who knew that these words were the best prescription to heal hurting human souls in the world.

It didn't take me too long to decide. I texted my reply to Matthew, "Luke 15:20". This verse reads:

So he got up and went to his father. But while he was still a long way off, his father saw him and was filled with compassion for him and he ran to his son, threw his arms around him and kissed him.

Within the verse itself, I believe that Dad would probably have identified the words about the father being filled with compassion and running towards his wayward boy. This description of God used to cause Dad's eyes to fill with tears--tears of joy at such an image. God's love for His children is so intense that he gives us freedom, never stops waiting for us to return when we wander, and then runs towards us when we turn back.

Not only did my father love these words but he also lived them. As one who first received the grace of our Lord, Dad then realized that it was his job to imitate it. So his eyes were always on the horizon looking for anyone who might not know or feel like they were beloved. He looked for people who had been hurt by the Church; who were marginalized by society or organized religion; who carried doubts, skepticism, and anger towards God; and yes, people who were wandering and lost. He was always looking and always moving towards them when he saw them. And he always approached and tried to embrace them with the love of the father in the parable—and he was good at it.

At the end of the day, this became the distinguishing mark of his life, and he touched thousands of souls I'll never know about because he did it everywhere he went.

The word "prodigal" means to be wastefully or recklessly extravagant, and people who have traditionally read the parable equate the word to the son. Others, though, have pointed out that it's the reckless extravagance of the loving father that's the real story. It takes a recklessly extravagant kind of father to give the boy freedom to sow wild oats…and then to spend all his days pacing the front porch waiting…and then to sprint toward the gaunt, broken (but familiar) figure coming up the driveway and then to shower him with rings, robe, fatted-calf, and party --when none of it was deserved. The father in the story was recklessly extravagant in his posture of love and grace—and the father in my story was the same. I had a prodigal dad and for the gift of his life and love I will forever be grateful! He taught us all well.

So when you see my nephew Matthew next time, tell him you heard that he lied. He said he was getting a "small" tattoo to remember Grandpa. It's not small. In fact, it's huge. Ask him to roll up his right sleeve and there on his strong right bicep you'll see that he is carrying words that describe the heart of my dad—and the heart of our family—and, oh yes, also the heart of God...Luke 15:20.

Thanks, Dad, for pointing us to this Good News from above that has the power to change everything.

Made in the USA
Middletown, DE
27 December 2015